A History of
Thunderbolt, Georgia

A History of
Thunderbolt, Georgia

by
LUCIANA M. SPRACHER

Thunderbolt, Georgia
2003

A History of Thunderbolt, Georgia
By Luciana Spracher

Copyright © 2003 by Thunderbolt Museum Society
ISBN 0-9729899-2-7

Designed by Stephen Hoffius
Cover design by Paul F. Rossmann

For additional copies of this book,
or for more information on the history of Thunderbolt,
please contact:
Thunderbolt Museum Society
2702 Mechanics Avenue
Thunderbolt, Georgia 31404
(912) 351-0836

THIS BOOK IS DEDICATED

TO THE PEOPLE OF THUNDERBOLT

IN MEMORY OF OUR PAST GENERATIONS

IN HONOR OF OUR PRESENT GENERATION

AND

IN HOPE FOR OUR FUTURE GENERATIONS

Acknowledgements

Thunderbolt's history dates back to Native Americans encamping along the bluff that overlooks the Wilmington River. However, the first documented history comes with Oglethorpe's landing at Savannah in 1733. Many individual Thunderboltians have collected information and artifacts on town and family history, however this information has never had a home except with that individual. Over the years many have expressed a desire to have a place open to the public to display Thunderbolt's history, but until now it has only been a dream.

With the new millennium came a new interest in achieving this dream. Funding, of course, for such a project was and is a major concern. Led by Joan Cesaroni, the Thunderbolt Town Council approached the State of Georgia through State Senator Regina Thomas and State Representative Lester Jackson for financial support for the undertaking. Both Thomas and Jackson greeted the idea with enthusiasm and obtained grants for the support of a museum from the state for the last three years. The Town Council continued their support of the endeavor, supplying a building and administering the grant monies.

Patty Dwyer McKenna had a dream and the determination to develop a historical society and the first meetings of the Thunderbolt Museum Society were scheduled. This book, the museum's physical property and displays, and the paperwork required to make the dream a reality can all be attributed to Patty. Without her inspiration and hard work, this project would have failed in the first year.

Our thanks to
Patty Dwyer McKenna

Thunderbolt Town Council
James Petrea, Mayor
Joan Cesaroni
John Hall
Frank Hardeman
John McKenna
Carl Smith
Joann Wotring
Anna Maria Thomas
Ernest Brown
Beth Goette
Bobby Hardman

Georgia State Representative Lester Jackson
Georgia State Senator Regina Thomas

The State of Georgia

Charter Members of the Thunderbolt Museum Society
& those who give so freely of their time.

This book is a beginning. As we delve into Thunderbolt's history, there will be subsequent editions, for we have barely begun the venture.

Table of Contents

A History of
Thunderbolt, Georgia

Introduction

The Town of Thunderbolt, located along the Wilmington River in coastal Georgia, has a rich and varied past. The small community has gone through a series of rebirths and regenerations as it has adapted to the changes in politics, culture, and environment. The town's relationship to the river has been the uniting tie between the different periods in its history. The position along the intra-coastal waterway, leading from the Atlantic Ocean to the City of Savannah, made Thunderbolt an important strategic defense point for the Native Americans, the colonial settlers, French forces during the American Revolution, the Confederate Army during the Civil War, and finally the United States Navy and Coast Guard during World War II. During times of peace, the location on the river promoted the area as a resort for Savannahians seeking an escape to cool breezes and summer fun along the Thunderbolt bluff. As Thunderbolt's resort industry was declining, due to the widespread use of the automobile, an explosion of the shrimping industry resulted in the community we know today. Thunderbolt became a thriving fishing village with a family-oriented community. The decline of the fishing industry in the late twentieth century created a shift back to a recreational community dependent upon an outside source of income from visitors enjoying its seafood and river life. As the town enters a new phase in its life, a look back at Thunderbolt's past demonstrates the community's resiliency and points towards a future regeneration.

CHAPTER ONE
The Naming and Location of Thunderbolt

The Legend of Thunderbolt
Before colonial settlement of Georgia, Thunderbolt was a small Native American village. Though abandoned by its Native American inhabitants before the colonists arrived, their influence remains even today in the defining and unique name of the town. The name comes from an Indian legend which relates the story of a severe storm during which "a thunderbolt from the heavens opened up a spring of fresh water and the place long afterwards smelled of the bolt."[1] The burnt smell has since been identified as a mixture of sulphur and iron found in the area's springs. It is thought that the spring of the legend was located on Tuberson Avenue and flowed until the 1920s. The development of Daffin Park caused a drop in the local water table and many of Thunderbolt's springs ceased to flow.[2]

The legend of the thunderbolt strike was perpetuated by General James Oglethorpe who heard the story from the Indian chief Tomo-chi-chi. The first recorded mention of the name Thunderbolt appears to be on 13 March 1733, when receipt was made of "a cask of potash made at Thunderbolt, in Georgia,"[3] produced by Samuel Baker, a merchant. Despite several official names over the years, the name of Thunderbolt has persevered and the legend has become a source of pride, tying the community to its Native American beginnings.[4]

Thunderbolt and the River

The Native Americans used the Thunderbolt settlement as a lookout point on the river. Thunderbolt's location on the river would ensure its future importance for colonial settlement. Located about five miles southeast of Savannah on a high bluff overlooking the Wilmington River, the town occupies a prime vantage point.[5]

The river below Thunderbolt Bluff has been referred to in history by many names. Connecting with the St. Augustine or Augustine Creek to the north and Wassaw Sound to the southeast, the river has carried both these names. Earliest records refer to it as Augustine Creek, which is now generally considered to be the smaller passage between the Savannah River and the Wilmington River, well north of Thunderbolt. Wassaw Sound, which opens into the Atlantic Ocean, and Wassaw Island retain their original Indian names. The river below the Thunderbolt Bluff was referred to as both Wassaw River and the anglicized version of Warsaw throughout the late 18th, 19th, and early 20th centuries. During the 20th century the river became known as the Wilmington River, named for nearby Wilmington Island, but many commonly refer to the stretch below the bluff as the Thunderbolt River (see Map 1).[6]

Despite the variation in name, the river is the defining characteristic of Thunderbolt, providing transportation, protection, pleasure, food and industry. The river was a lifeline that carried the community from colonial settlement through the next two and half centuries.[7]

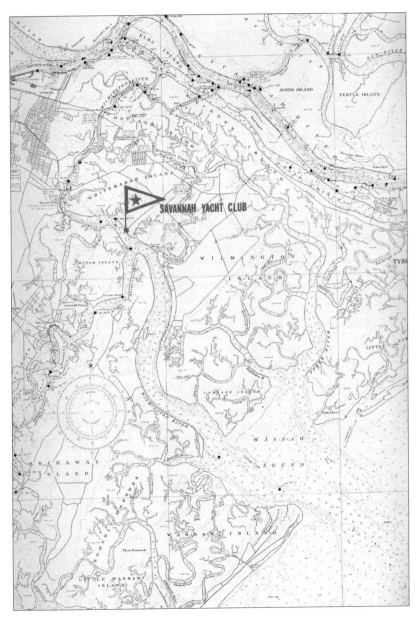

Map 1: Coastal Waters off of Thunderbolt and Savannah
"Savannah Yacht Club" (1969)
Vertical File: Societies & Clubs-Yacht Club Vertical File
Georgia Historical Society, Savannah, Georgia

CHAPTER TWO
Colonial Settlement of Thunderbolt

Oglethorpe's Military Outpost System

Thunderbolt gained new importance in the 1730s with the British colonization of Georgia. Led by General James Oglethorpe, a variety of colonists settled in Savannah in 1733. Oglethorpe represented the Trustees for the Establishment of the Colony of Georgia in England. The Trustees had high hopes of developing a Utopian colony, minus the slavery, rum, and land greed seen in the colonies to the north. Though the major settlement in Georgia was to be Savannah, Oglethorpe developed numerous smaller settlements in an "agrarian-military outpost scheme to protect the settlement of Savannah from the Spanish."[8]

Along with Thunderbolt, these outposts included Hampstead, Highgate, Abercorn, Acton and Joseph's Town. Oglethorpe's emphasis on town planning in Savannah was echoed in these smaller settlements and eighteenth-century maps suggest Thunderbolt may have had a town plan as well. However, Thunderbolt's development during the 19th and 20th centuries has left no evidence of an original town plan. The earliest known map showing Thunderbolt was published by Samuel Urlsperger in "Ausfuhrlicke Nachricht Vod den Saltzburgishen Emigranten" in 1735 (see Map 2). Urlsperger's map shows the plan of Savannah and the surrounding and supporting outposts including Thunderbolt, depicted by a flag and radiating lines alongside Augustine Creek. The majority of these small settle-

Map 2: "A Map of the County of Savannah," Samuel Urlsperger, c1735
Waring Map Collection MS 1018, Volume 1, Plate 7
Georgia Historical Society, Savannah, Georgia

ments disappeared after a short period due to poor agricultural conditions. However, Thunderbolt's prime location on the intra-coastal waterway ensured its continued importance to the Colony of Georgia.[9]

Oglethorpe chose the former Native American site as a settlement to provide a defense against southeastern access to the City of Savannah. Thunderbolt was on the inland water route which led from Savannah south to St. Simon's Island and Spanish Florida. Oglethorpe established defenses along this route in the event of a Spanish invasion. Early detection of intruders by these outposts could provide Savannah residents with the necessary time to prepare themselves for defense. Settlements at Thunderbolt and Skidaway Island were established within the first year of the settlement of Georgia for this reason. Oglethorpe built Fort Frederica on St. Simon's Island in 1736 as his southernmost defense, and it became the southern anchor of this defense strategy.[10]

In 1736, two constables were stationed at the "fortified farming village,"[11] of Thunderbolt. General Oglethorpe continued to check on Thunderbolt's progress after colonists had been installed, emphasizing its importance in his strategic system. He often stopped at the settlement on his trips south to Darien and St. Simons Island. In February 1735, he informed the Trustees in England of Thunderbolt's development, declaring it "in a very good situation."[12]

Thunderbolt's Colonial Settlers

John Percival[13], the Earl of Egmont, recorded the minutes of the meetings of the Trustees for the Establishment of the Colony of Georgia, who oversaw the planning of the colony and the distribution of land and resources to potential settlers. Thunderbolt's colonial settlement and the role Roger Lacey played in its development can be traced through the minutes. On 24 May 1732, Lacey presented a proposal to the Trustees to accompany twenty charity children to Georgia for use in the production of silk. Sericulture in Georgia was of great importance to the Trustees, who hoped that a successful silk industry would ensure Georgia's success and importance as a British colony, encouraging increased financial support by investors and the Crown. Lacey, with his brother James, brothers Theophilus and Joseph Hetherington, and Philip Bishop formed a company in 1732 to carry on the silk industry in the new colony.[14]

Though the Trustees encouraged Lacey's idea, the children's parents objected and the plan fell apart. After this there is no indication in the Trustees' minutes that Lacey and his partners were involved in sericulture, though it is likely that they planted mulberry trees (used in the cultivation of silk worms) once they arrived in Georgia to satisfy the Trustees. Early grants in the Colony of Georgia stipulated that all grantees plant a certain number of mulberry trees per each five-hundred acre tract. It is more than likely that Lacey used the prospect of silk production to further his interests with the Trustees in hopes of acquiring land in the new colony.[15]

After the dismissal of the plan utilizing the children, Lacey addressed the Trustees in December 1732, announcing that he "desired for himself and four other persons five hundred acres of land in Georgia each, carrying over with them each man four servants." Two weeks after the request, on 21 December 1732, the Trustees granted Roger Lacey, James Lacey, Joseph Hetherington and Philip Bishop each country lots of five-hundred acres along the Thunderbolt Bluff. On 28 March 1733, some of the grantees and their families accompanied by a total of thirty servants, set sail from England on the ship *Pearl*, piloted by Captain Coram.[16]

On 4 July 1733, Joseph Hetherington's brothers, Theophilus and Robert, each received grants of two-hundred and fifty acres in Thunderbolt, bringing the total original Trustee grants in Thunderbolt to 2,500 acres. The new village along the bluff was now characterized by three distinct family settlements, that of the Lacey brothers, the Hetherington brothers, and Philip Bishop's family.[17]

The Laceys

The clear leader of the group in England and once the group settled in Georgia was Roger Lacey. Roger Hugh Lacey was born on 24 June 1706 in London, England. He became a merchant and was one of the stewards of the Grand Lodge of Masons. On 1 February 1734, Lacey arrived in Georgia with his wife and son to settle his new land.[18]

Lacey had been preceded on the journey by his mother, Elizabeth Lacey, who arrived in Georgia on 14 January 1734. Unfortunately, Elizabeth died only six months later on 1 August 1734. Lacey's brother, James, also a recipient of a five-hundred acre tract, died shortly after arriving in the new colony, leaving Roger Lacey in control of his land as well.[19]

By December of 1736 Lacey was well settled on his land. Once at Thunderbolt, Lacey experimented in the production of potash, encouraged by Samuel Baker's earlier success. Lacey cleared a large portion of his property, which he called "Oakland," and planted Indian corn and grain. John Wesley, clergyman of the Church of England and later founder of Methodism, formed a close friendship with Lacey. Wesley often stopped at Lacey's home in Thunderbolt on his circuit route to preach to the settlers and Indians. Wesley is said to have preached under the oaks along the Thunderbolt Bluff.[20]

Lacey's influence did not end with his leadership at Thunderbolt. In 1735, Thomas Thynne, Lord Viscount Weymouth and Grand Master of the Grand Lodge in England, appointed Roger Lacey the Provincial Grand Master of Masons in the Province of Georgia. Lacey is considered the "Father of Freemasonry in Georgia." His role was commemorated by a historical marker along the Thunderbolt Bluff, which was unveiled on 2 March 1956 during the town's centennial celebration. A local Masonic lodge bears his name as well.[21]

General Oglethorpe relied on Lacey to help settle the new town of Augusta, established in 1736 northwest of Savannah. In June 1736, surveyor Noble Jones laid out the new town along the

Savannah River, which would serve as a trading post for Indian traders. As in Savannah, Oglethorpe established an organized town plan utilizing a center square surrounded by public lots, forty one-acre house lots and a six-hundred acre common. Oglethorpe appointed Lacey to establish the trading post at Mores' Fort and distribute the fifty-acre lots outside of the main town "to those he saw fit." Lacey used ten of his own servants in the construction of the new fort and served as the Captain of Militia at Augusta. Lacey further aided the Trustees by serving as an "Agent to the Indian Nation twice" in 1737.[22]

On 1 August 1737, Lacey returned to Savannah from Augusta but died only two days later. Lacey was buried with full military honors on his property at Thunderbolt. After his death, Lacey's widow became involved with Theophilus Hetherington and married him on 1 December 1739.[23]

The Hetheringtons and Bishop

The remaining settlers of Thunderbolt are shrouded in controversy. Left without Lacey's guidance, it seems that they let the settlement decline and became engaged in illegal activities which led them to flee the colony.

Joseph Hetherington, the first of the three Hetherington brothers to receive a Thunderbolt grant, took possession of his property on 7 July 1733 and was well settled by that September. Little is known of his activities until July 1738 when he was convicted, with Robert and Philip Bishop, of felony for killing Henry Parker's hogs and cattle for his own use. The Hetheringtons and Bishop were also involved in smuggling rum into Savannah, which was prohibited during the early period of Georgia's colonization under the Trustees. The three were incarcerated in Savannah on the livestock charges and on 25 July 1738 escaped and fled the colony. This left all of the Hetherington land in the control of Theophilus and the Lacey brothers' land in that of the widow Lacey. After fleeing to Carolina, Joseph died in 1740. Theophilus Hetherington and the widow Lacey left the colony in

1740 due to debts, abandoning all of the original grants. They followed his brothers to Carolina, where Mrs. Lacey died in 1740.[24]

Colonial Fortification and Farms

The settlement of Thunderbolt, comprising a total of 2,500 acres, consisted of one-hundred acres of cleared land and a fortified village of settlers' homes built within a palisade fort. While settlement at Thunderbolt was mainly part of the defense strategy against the Spanish, the fort also guarded the settlers against potential Indian attacks on the frontier of Georgia. The fort was armed with cannon manned by a nightly guard of the settlers and servants. The log fort, built in 1734, had fallen into disrepair by 1737 with the absence of Lacey.[25]

The Trustees noted the progress of the settlers at Thunderbolt in one of their meetings in September of 1737:

> *Near one-hundred acres of land cleared, three houses which are musket proof, and a small fort which was mounted with nine guns: But part of the walls are now fallen which the rest will soon follow.*[26]

All progress at Thunderbolt was centered around the efforts of Roger Lacey. He was the most industrious of all the Thunderbolt settlers. Sixty of all of the cleared acres, more than half the total, were on his property. Lacey erected "a very handsome house,"[27] and had eleven servants working for him. Though the production of potash did not prove successful, Lacey led the settlers in planting and supplementing their income by "sawing timber for the sugar islands and splitting staves to go to Madeira."[28] The journal of William Stephens[29] confirms that Lacey was responsible for Thunderbolt's advancement and that "the improvements of Hetherington and Bishop are very little."[30]

Colonial Abandonment

Without Lacey's leadership, first due to his absence and new role in Augusta and then to his death, the promising colonial settlement of Thunderbolt began a fast decline. It has been argued that Oglethorpe, mastermind of the outpost settlements, contributed to Thunderbolt's demise by sending Lacey to Augusta when he was so desperately needed in Thunderbolt. By the summer of 1738, Thunderbolt's abandonment was evident: "Thunderbolt...that village, once the great exemplar of all improvements in these parts,...in a manner become desolate..."[31]

When Theophilus Hetherington and the widow Lacey left in 1740, the last of the original settlers were gone and the village was abandoned for the second time. The large tracts of five-hundred acres were divided into farm lots of forty-five and fifty acre increments and were designated as parts of the 1st, 2nd, 3rd, and 4th Tythings of Reynolds Ward. Two-hundred and fifty acres were set aside in 1743 for former indentured servants. The premise behind the so-called "Servants Lands" was that the former servants "might have encouragement given them to go upon and cultivate the land."[32]

The strategic importance of Thunderbolt was not forgotten during this redistribution of land. In 1742, William Stephens noted that a watch had been sent to Thunderbolt and settlers in the area were instructed to fire the cannon on the bluff to warn Savannah of an emergency. Stephens provided settlers with arms and ammunition to defend themselves against enemy attack.[33]

Thunderbolt and the Royal Colony of Georgia

In 1752, the Trustees' charter for the Colony of Georgia expired and the colony was taken over by the Crown. The new government implemented in Georgia, led by a Royal Governor, eased many of the former restrictions established by the Trustees in their effort to create an ideal society, resulting in a new era of development and settlement in Georgia. Plantations became more prominent with the use of slave labor and began to overshadow the smaller landowners and farmers.

The Servants Lands had been kept separate from the farm lots, but by 1765 were combined under the ownership of two men. The original 2,500 acres, granted to the Laceys, Hetheringtons, and Bishop, were reunited under the ownership of Governor Ellis and Grey Elliott. In 1759, Governor Henry Ellis, the first Royal Governor of Georgia, petitioned the Crown for three-hundred acres in the 3rd and 4th Tythings of Reynolds Ward in Thunderbolt.[34]

Grey Elliott was a partner in the firm of Elliott & Gordon and a prominent Georgian at the time. He purchased the farm lots of John Graham (granted to him in 1759) and set out to acquire all the land in the 1st, 2nd, 3rd, and 4th Tythings Reynolds Ward not already owned by Ellis. By 1765, Elliott had purchased farm lots of James Edward Powell, Michael Switzer, a shipbuilder, William Bell, a carpenter from Beaufort, Charles Watson, Robert Williams, and David Montaigate, among others. Elliott called the total, about four-hundred and sixty acres, "Greenwich." In addition, he acquired three-hundred acres of pine formerly part of the Servants Lands in 1762.[35]

In 1765, Elliott sold Greenwich to Samuel Bowen, and two-hundred and forty-five acres of the pine lands to Claudia Mulryne. Bowen raised Sago palms at Greenwich and in 1768 he received a King's Patent for his Sago Powder. Bowen was a supplier of Sago, which could be used as a food source, to the British Royal Navy. It is probable that Greenwich was also the first Georgia plantation to produce soybeans.[36]

The Mulrynes combined the pine lands with their plantation "Bonaventure."[37] Claudia and her husband, John, had settled at Bonaventure in 1765. John Mulryne operated large sawmills throughout coastal Georgia and owned a great deal of land, including "Placentia" plantation south of Thunderbolt. "The Cottage," a small plantation of only eight acres, was carved from the Bonaventure tract for the Mulryne's daughter, Mary. Mary lived there with her husband, Josiah Tattnall. The Cottage was the only plantation actually located in Thunderbolt, though all of the plantations in the area, Bonaventure, Greenwich, and Placentia, play a role its history. The Cottage plantation was small by all standards and provided only garden products. Part of the Cottage property was the site of the Savannah Yacht Club built in the 1880s in Thunderbolt.[38]

By the outbreak of the American Revolutionary War, Thunderbolt had evolved from a colonial settlement with small subsistence farming into a system of plantations. The politics of the plantation owners would play a role in the war with Bowen supporting the American patriots, and the Tattnalls and Mulrynes supporting the British Loyalists.[39]

CHAPTER THREE
Thunderbolt and the American Revolution

The Occupation of Savannah

In 1778, the British shifted the focus of their war strategy from the northern colonies to the southern colonies, recognizing that the American colonies were weaker along this front. The Chief Commander of the British forces, Sir Henry Clinton, planned an attack on Savannah, a vital port, for the winter of 1778. British troops left from New York and St. Augustine to meet and capture the important southern city. Though the flank from St. Augustine did not arrive in time, aided by area Loyalists the British moved into Savannah virtually unopposed. Arriving on 24 December 1778, the British had control of the city by 29 December. However, the surrounding areas, including Thunderbolt, remained under the patriots' control. The human toll of the seizure included seven British killed and nineteen British wounded and five-hundred American soldiers either captured or killed.[40]

D'Estaing's Headquarters and Hospital
& The Siege of Savannah

In September 1779, Count Charles Henri D'Estaing, the French naval commander, arrived in the port of Savannah with a force of twenty-two ships and four thousand troops to join forces with the Americans to drive the British under General Prevost out of Savannah and Georgia. American General Benjamin Lincoln mustered fifteen-thousand men to join with the French forces for a combined attack on the British in October 1779.[41]

On 12 September 1779, D'Estaing and his troops landed at Beaulieu, a plantation thirteen miles south of Savannah owned by Mr. Morel, from which to march into the city. A second landing at Thunderbolt was proposed by Levi Sheftall[42], who supplied the French forces with maps and information and later led the French from Thunderbolt to Spring Hill Redoubt.[43]

In October, D'Estaing seized Bonaventure plantation and set up his headquarters. John Mulryne, the owner of Bonaventure, was an English colonel and had remained loyal to the British Crown. In 1776, he had helped the last Royal Governor, James Wright, escape Savannah to Cockspur Island, where the two fled the colony on the English man-of-war *Scarborough*. The plantation house was converted into a military hospital and Thunderbolt served as the point of communication with the French fleet. Several French maps, including that drawn by French engineer Antoine O'Connor (see Map 3), show "Tunder Blutt," or Thunderbolt, and the hospital along a route from the eastern edge of the town of Thunderbolt.[44]

The Siege of Savannah, the attack of the French and Americans against the British, lasted only about one hour, occurring along the western boundary of the city.[45] The Siege was a failure. The French lost one-hundred and fifty men and three-hundred and seventy were wounded. The American casualties were tallied at two-hundred and thirty killed or wounded, while the British lost only eighteen with forty wounded. The Battle of Bunker Hill was the only military conflict in the American Revolutionary War to exceed the combined casualties of the Siege of Savannah.[46]

D'Estaing was wounded by small musket balls in his left arm and above his left breast. He recovered at the hospital at

Opposite: Map 3: Map of Savannah during the Siege of Savannah, Antoine O'Connor, c1779
Waring Map Collection MS 1018, Volume 3, Plate 22
Georgia Historical Society, Savannah, Georgia

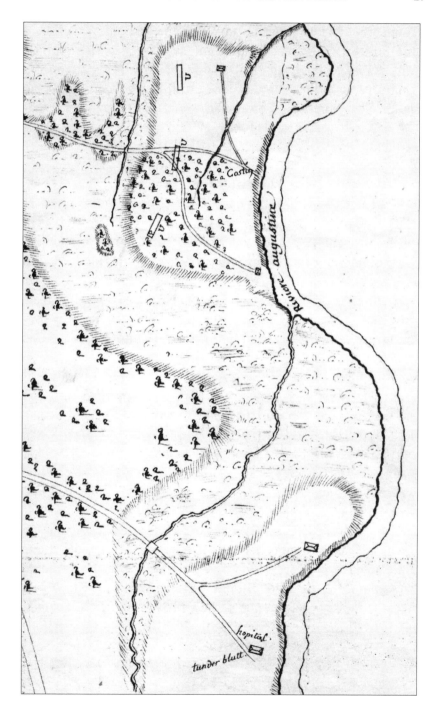

Thunderbolt before returning with his forces to France. It is likely that those French soldiers who died at the hospital on Bonaventure were buried on the plantation. The French forces departed from Thunderbolt and Causton's Bluff, north of Thunderbolt on the river. The liberation of Savannah would not occur for another two and half years until 11 July 1782, after the British surrendered at Yorktown on 19 October 1781.[47]

Local Plantations after the War

When Georgia was taken back from British control in 1782, the Treason and Confiscation Act of 1778 was implemented by the State of Georgia. The properties of the Mulrynes and Tattnalls, Loyalist sympathizers, were confiscated and Bonaventure was sold at public auction to John Habersham on 13 June 1782. Captain Mulryne, who had earlier fled to New Providence, Nassau, Bahamas, died on 7 January 1786. His son-in-law, Josiah Tattnall, and his family went to England and settled in London.[48]

Josiah Tattnall, Jr. (d. 6 June 1803), fought for the Americans under General Nathaniel Greene and was able to buy back the family plantation from Habersham on 10 May 1785. Josiah Tattnall, Jr. became an influential and prominent citizen of the new State of Georgia.[49] He served as a State Senator and in 1801 was elected Governor of Georgia. Tattnall has also been credited with the introduction of island cotton from the Bahamas into Georgia.[50]

An early map of Savannah, drawn by John McKinnon circa 1800 (see Map 4), shows the area of Thunderbolt, along what is at this time referred to as the Warsaw River, and Bonaventure to the north of Thunderbolt. Augustine Creek now refers to the narrower branch of the river, further north, connecting with the Savannah River.[51]

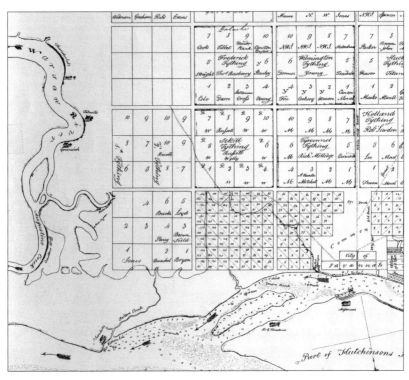

Map 4: Plan of Savannah, Georgia, John McKinnon, c1800
Waring Map Collection MS 1018, Volume 2, Plate 4
Georgia Historical Society, Savannah, Georgia

CHAPTER FOUR
Antebellum Thunderbolt

Plantations and Farms

The first half of the nineteenth century in Thunderbolt continued to be characterized by the large, neighboring plantations and small, subsistence farmers scattered in the area. The Herb family owned land at Thunderbolt and had several buildings along the bluff. In 1784, John McQueen, Sr. purchased The Cottage, and his son, John McQueen, Jr. settled at Causton's Bluff, north of Thunderbolt on the bluff.[52]

Thunderbolt's neighboring plantations also changed ownership during the early 1800s. John P. Williamson, who was elected Mayor of Savannah in November of 1808, operated the thirteen-hundred acre Placentia plantation. After being held by Dr. Beecroft in the late 1790s, Greenwich was acquired by John Morel before he died in 1802.[53]

Commodore Josiah Tattnall, descendent of the earlier Tattnall, sold six-hundred acres of Bonaventure to Peter Wiltberger on 10 March 1846. Wiltberger, a prominent Savannah businessman, set aside seventy acres of the land in the northeast corner of the tract for a public cemetery. The new cemetery was operated by the Evergreen Company of Bonaventure under the direction of Wiltberger. On 12 June 1868, Wiltberger's son, Major William H. Wiltberger, organized the Evergreen Cemetery Company to regulate the sale of the cemetery lots and manage the perpetual care of the plots, paid for by the families.

The City of Savannah purchased the Evergreen Cemetery of Bonaventure for $30,000 on 7 July 1907. The cemetery, at one-hundred and sixty acres, became known as Bonaventure Cemetery and continues to be maintained by the City of Savannah. In 1936, the city purchased Greenwich plantation from Dr. H. N. Torrey of Detroit as an addition to the expanding Bonaventure Cemetery.[54]

Little is known about the activities or residents in Thunderbolt at this time. However, Thunderbolt remained an important point on the intra-coastal waterway, as the chief entrance from the barrier islands into Savannah and the mainland. John McKinnon's 1823 map of nearby Liberty Island (housed in the collections of the Georgia Historical Society) depicts a public landing on the bluff near property of the Herb family. The Pest House was at Thunderbolt around 1846, and is believed to be where the sick and indigent were quarantined. It was later removed from the area in 1877.[55]

Incorporation of Warsaw, 1856

By the 1850s, Thunderbolt as a village was on the rise. On 3 March 1856 the village was incorporated by an act of the General Assembly of the State of Georgia as the Town of Warsaw. The legislation outlined the following:

> *That from and after this passage of this act, all of that bluff, or parcel of land situated, lying and being in the county of Chatham, and on the Warsaw river, extending from marsh to marsh, at either terminus, the same being about half of a mile in distance on the Warsaw river, and extending back from said river half a mile from either terminus, which was originally called O'Bryansville, but more recently Thunderbolt, shall hereafter be called, known and designated as the town of Warsaw.[56]*

The reference to O'Bryansville is rare, but for a brief period Thunderbolt was called O'Bryansville after a William O'Bryan who owned property along the river.

The new name was taken from the Warsaw River along which the town was located. Warsaw refers to the Indian name of Wassaw, as in Wassaw Sound and Wassaw Island. The new name did not catch on and residents of the area continued to refer to the community as Thunderbolt. However, the river was consistently called the Warsaw River throughout the nineteenth century.[57]

CHAPTER FIVE

Thunderbolt Battery and the Civil War

Oglethorpe's system of outposts, which had served as a defensive shield for the City of Savannah, was resurrected during the Civil War by the Confederate States of America Army. Fort Pulaski, the federal fort constructed on Cockspur Island in the 1840s, was seized by Confederate forces in 1861 and was thought to be Savannah's most important defense against enemies entering from the Atlantic Ocean. However, when Fort Pulaski fell in April of 1862 to rifle cannon, smaller earthworks defending the water approaches around Savannah became the real defense.[58]

In 1874, Georgia historian Charles C. Jones, Jr. described the Confederate defenses as:

> ... *an interior line of forts and water batteries which, commencing with Fort Jackson and the Savannah River batteries, included Fort Barstow, works at Causton's Bluff and on Whitemarsh Island, batteries at Greenwich, Thunderbolt, the Isle of Hope, and at Beaulieu, and rested its right on the Rose Dew batteries.*[59]

These earthworks, including Thunderbolt, created an interior line of defense to support the advanced line, which included the larger fortifications of Fort Pulaski, Wilmington Island, Green Island, and Fort McAllister. Fort Jackson served as the Confederate Army's headquarters for the smaller batteries. Communications between the river batteries was maintained by telegraph and sema- phore flag signaling.[60]

Along the Warsaw River, Fort Thunderbolt, or Thunder- bolt Battery as it was more commonly called, was constructed to guard against attack coming in from the Wassaw Sound. A sketch of the Thunderbolt Battery shows the earthworks along the river with numerous mounds, a bombproof shelter, and cannon and guns strategically positioned along the bluff guarding the river (see Map 5, Figures 1 and 2). In addition, large live oaks were placed in the river below the bluff to create obstacles and slow down enemy ships trying to move up the river towards Savan- nah. W. A. Webb commanded the Confederate naval squadron from the *C.S.S. Atlanta* off of Thunderbolt in 1863; and the *C.S.S. Oconee* was also stationed near Thunderbolt for a time.[61]

Several contemporary descriptions of Thunderbolt Bat- tery emphasize its importance and describe its location. On 1 December 1861, in his personal diary, Cornelius R. Hanleiter described the state of the battery:

> *The Rifle men [Phoenix Riflemen] are in charge*
> *of the Battery at Thunderbolt—five large guns—*
> *and seem to be very comfortably quartered. They*
> *have a beautiful location, on a high bluff, com-*
> *manding the river at this point.*[62]

The *Philadelphia Enquirer* announced the strategic importance of the Thunderbolt Battery and the desire of the Union forces to gain control of it on 7 February 1862:

> *...having four guns and located on the water ap-*
> *proach from Wassaw Sound up the Wilmington*
> *River. And if in their [Union] possession, they*

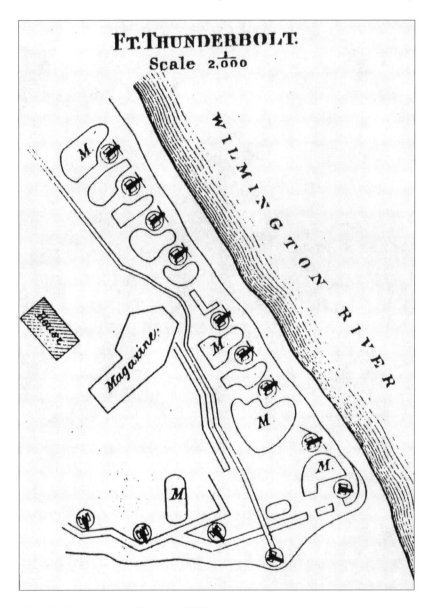

Map 5: Thunderbolt Battery, 1865
Philadelphia: Bowen & Co., Lithographers, 1865
Civil War Maps, Geography & Map Division, Library of Congress

Figure 1: Thunderbolt Battery
Lamas, Claudia B. "Fortification Survey of Savannah River and Area
Waterways, Savannah, Georgia 1861-1865." TMs (photocopy). Minis
Room, Lane Library, Armstrong Atlantic State University, Savannah,
Georgia, Figure 4.

*could land 20,000 men and march them into the
South.*[63]

Apparently several unsuccessful attempts were made by
the Federal soldiers to land at the Thunderbolt Battery. On 19

Figure 2: Thunderbolt Battery Looking Down River, William Waud, 1865
Harper's Weekly (21 January 1865)
Prints & Photographs Division, Library of Congress

May 1862, the local newspaper reported one such attempt: "Last Saturday night at Thunderbolt, more Yankees attempted to land, and were fired upon by our pickets. None of our men were injured."[64]

Guns at the Thunderbolt Battery included 8" Columbiads, 7" rifled guns, mortars, 8" Navy guns, 18 pounders, 24 pounders, 42 pounders, and 32 pounders. In March of 1862, the Skidaway Battery was abandoned and its guns were taken to Thunderbolt to strengthen the battery. In March of 1863 the Thunderbolt Battery was once again strengthened with additional guns. It was recorded on 31 March 1863 by Colonel T. Gorgas, the Chief of Ordnance, that the Thunderbolt Battery now had a total of fourteen guns.[65]

In October 1863, Confederate States of America President, Jefferson Davis, toured the river forts and batteries on the steamer *Beauregard*. At Thunderbolt he disembarked to inspect the Phoenix Riflemen. The Phoenix Riflemen were one of the oldest volunteer militia companies in Savannah and maintained guard at the Thunderbolt Battery during the Civil War as part of the 63rd Georgia Regiment.[66]

In 1864, Union gunboats were anchored off of Thunderbolt. A Union private aboard one wrote, "It looks to me like the Confederate States is compelled to starve in a short time."[67] Thunderbolt never fell to the enemy however, and increased armament and river obstructions kept the Union forces from landing. It was the advance of Union troops on Fort McAllister by land that led to the evacuation of Savannah and Thunderbolt Battery. "After having spiked the guns and destroyed the carriages and ammunition,"[68] the garrisons of Thunderbolt, under Colonel Edward C. Anderson, evacuated to Fort Jackson. There they joined the garrisons of Causton's Bluff and the Savannah River batteries on 20 December 1864 and were taken by steamer to Screven's Ferry to march into Hardeeville. After the abandonment of the Thunderbolt Battery, some of Sherman's troops departed from Thunderbolt for Beaufort to begin their campaign through the Carolinas.[69]

Nothing remains of the Thunderbolt Battery today due to a combination of initial neglect and commercial and industrial development. However, Thunderbolt's importance in local Civil War history is not forgotten.[70]

CHAPTER SIX
Thunderbolt, 1865-1900

By the time the Sanborn Insurance Company of New York made their first map of Thunderbolt, Georgia in 1888, the town already had numerous dwellings along the bluff of the Warsaw River. River Drive and the Coastline Railroad (discussed in Chapter Seven) paralleled the bluff, providing visitors from Savannah access to the boarding houses, including the Warsaw Inn and Restaurant and several docks and pavilions that dotted the banks of the river. The only industry apparent besides that of a small resort area was the terrapin farm, seen as terrapin pens along the southern edge of town. The terrapin raised at Thunderbolt could have been used by the local restaurants for stews or shipped north to larger hotels as Barbee at Isle of Hope did (see Map 6).[71]

The 1898 Sanborn Insurance Map reflects a boom for the town with many new dwellings, hotels and restaurants. The town was now supported by an engine house on River Drive that was equipped with a fifty-gallon supply tank and one hand engine, and depended on the work of fifty volunteer firemen. The Winthrop Company, manufacturers of "Rubberaid," had a large facility in Thunderbolt (see Map 8). The chief industry of tourism was steadily growing with sites like Bannon House, Varn & Byrd Music Park and Tivoli Park (see Map 7).[72]

Thunderbolt's Government
The first government of Thunderbolt was a commission

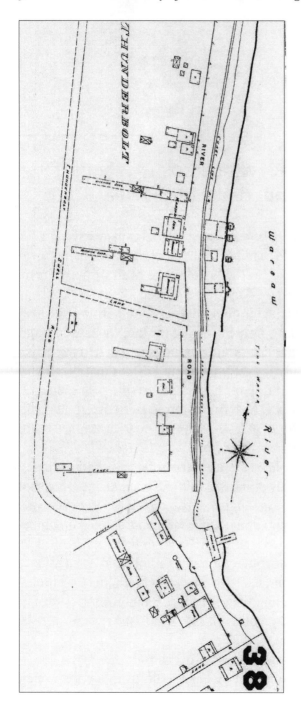

**Map 6: Thunder-
bolt, Georgia, 1888**
New York: Sanborn
Map & Publishing
Company, Ltd., 1888.

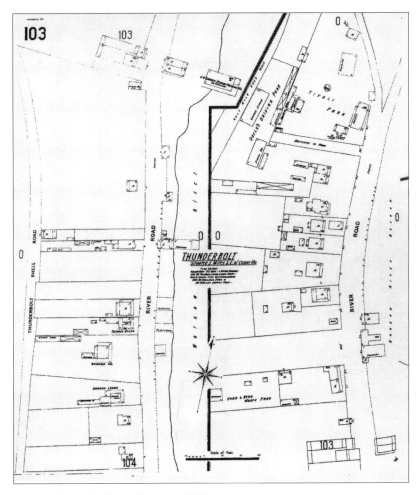

Map 7: Thunderbolt, Georgia, 1898
New York: Sanborn Map & Publishing Company, Ltd., 1898.

format comprising five men, one of whom also served as chairman of the commission. The first commission, consisting of Maxine Devergus, chairman, William Fennel, clerk, Henry Ambos, William Grey, and Randolf Paff, was elected on 16 March 1886 at the home of Edward Bannon. The first meeting of the commission was held at Henry Ambos' house in Thunderbolt. The commission government oversaw the affairs of the town from

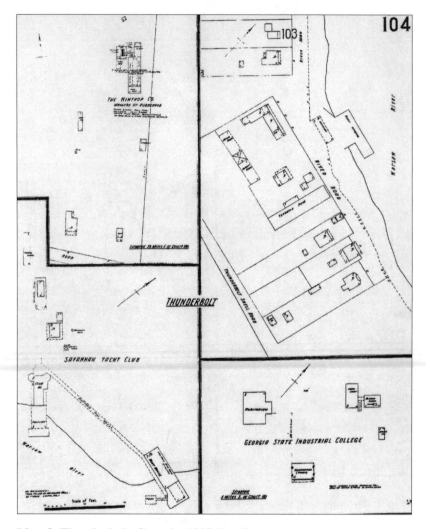

Map 8: Thunderbolt, Georgia, 1898-Details
New York: Sanborn Map & Publishing Company, Ltd., 1898.

1886 until 1902.[73]

At the same time the commission was organized, Thunderbolt's first jail was erected on a lot owned by Henry Ambos, at a cost of $161.83. The annual rental for the lot was $10.00. The first prisoner of the town was Richard Nichols, who given the choice of a $20.00 fine or thirty days in jail, chose the jail sentence. Mr. William Black served as the first town marshal in 1886, and worked only on Saturdays.[74]

Religion in Thunderbolt

In 1894, Miss Agnes "Aggie" Gray led a movement to establish an inter-denominational church at Thunderbolt. With funds collected for the purpose, a small building was erected by Mr. Gray on River Drive, along Thunderbolt's Bluff, in 1896. Miss Agnes Gray taught school during the week and held Sunday School on the weekends. The one-room frame schoolhouse had four double hung windows, with twelve over twelve panes, and an entrance on the gabled end of the structure.[75]

During the late 1800s, black residents in the community erected a prayer house, a branch of the First African Baptist Church of Savannah, on Bannon Drive at the end of Mechanics Avenue. On 3 January 1900, the prayer house reorganized as an independent church and changed its name from Thunderbolt First African Baptist Church to the Central Baptist Church.[76]

Georgia State Industrial College

Georgia State Industrial College, the first public institution of higher learning established in Georgia for blacks, was unusual because it was located adjacent to the white resort area of Thunderbolt, connected by the streetcar line from Savannah. However, the relationship between the school and community has always been amicable with the two acting as helping hands to each other.[77]

On 26 November 1890, an act of the Georgia Assembly resolved to "establish in connection with the State University, and forming one of the departments thereof, a school for the education and training of Negro students." Thus the Georgia State Industrial College for Colored Youths was born, a result of the Second Morrill Act of 1890 and one of the first Negro land-grant colleges. A preliminary session of the school was held in Athens, Georgia from June to August 1891, conducted by Principal

Figure 3: Georgia State Industrial College
Georgia Historical Society Photograph Collection VM 1361 PR, Box 2,
Folder 82
Georgia Historical Society, Savannah, Georgia

Richard R. Wright. In October 1891, Georgia State Industrial College moved five miles southeast of Savannah, onto the former plantation of Placentia, just south of Thunderbolt. Regular school sessions began at the Thunderbolt site that October (see Map 8).[78]

Major Richard R. Wright served as the first President of the college from 1891 until 1921. During its first thirty years the enrollment of the school increased from eight students to five-hundred and eighty-five students. The original campus consisted of eighty-six acres, fifty-one of which were farm and thirty-five campus. When founded, the school had only Boggs Hall, Parsons Hall and a farmhouse (see Figure 3 and Map 8). The Sanborn Insurance maps show the campus with two auditoriums (one two-stories and the other a three-story tabby building), a workshop, and a blacksmith shop.[79] Under Wright four new buildings were erected, including Meldrim Hall (1896), Hill Hall (1901), the Dairy Barn & Creamery (1904), and a complex including the

Figure 4: Georgia State Industrial College, 1937
Cordray-Foltz Collection VM 1360 PH, Box 3, Folder 26, Item 8
Georgia Historical Society, Savannah, Georgia

shoe repair shop, the laundry and the home economics building (1915). The initial educational program offered by Georgia State Industrial College included only agriculture and mechanical arts, as well as a four-year high school (see Figure 4).[80]

C. G. Wiley, Wright's successor, served as President from 1921 until 1926, Wiley admitted the first women students to the college and initiated regular summer sessions in 1922. Dr. Benjamin F. Hubert, President from 1926 to 1947, discontinued the high school and normal departments and transformed the school into a four-year college offering bachelors degrees in agriculture and home economics. In 1931, when the State University system was placed under a Board of Regents, the college began offering degree programs in English, natural sciences, social sciences, and business administration.[81]

During the 1930s and 1940s numerous buildings were added and on 18 January 1950 the school was renamed Savannah State College. By 1956, the year of Thunderbolt's centennial, the school had grown to one-hundred and thirty-six acres

Figure 5: Georgia State Industrial College, 1936
Cordray-Foltz Collection VM 1360 PH, Box 3, Folder 26, Item 5
Georgia Historical Society, Savannah, Georgia

with thirty buildings and was Georgia's largest institution for the
higher education of African Americans.[82]

CHAPTER SEVEN
Thunderbolt the River Resort

Thunderbolt's popularity as a river resort spanned the 19th century and the early 20th century. As early as 1850, the Mount Pleasant Retreat provided boats for tourists to go out on fishing parties. The Thunderbolt bluff had several hotels and guest cottages to accommodate Savannahians when they came to enjoy the cool breezes and entertainment along the river. Famous visitors to Thunderbolt included General Grant in 1880 while on a visit to Savannah. [83]

In 1875, Captain Threadcraft, owner of Greenwich plantation and the Thunderbolt Race Track, remodeled his famous Park House in Thunderbolt. The new additions included a restaurant, saloon and bowling alley. After Threadcraft leased the Park House to George Alley, the spot became known as Allies Wharf.[84]

By 1898, Thunderbolt boasted many of the area's most exciting attractions. In the northern section of town, Captain Threadcraft had built a horse race track and Tivoli Park was built next to the track with a bandstand, pavilion and restaurant. Music was one of the biggest draws to the small resort. The Casino, Tivoli Park, and Varn & Byrd Music Park all had pavilions and bandstands for outdoor concerts (see Map 7).[85]

Yachting in Thunderbolt
Sailing has been part of Savannah's culture since 1857.

Figure 6: Savannah Yacht Club seen from the Wilmington River
Georgia Historical Society Postcard Collection VM 1361 PC, Box 8
Georgia Historical Society, Savannah, Georgia

Figure 7: Savannah Yacht Club Clubhouse
Georgia Historical Society Postcard Collection VM 1361 PC, Box 8
Georgia Historical Society, Savannah, Georgia

The "golden age" of yachting in Savannah, roughly 1897 through 1906, revolved around the Savannah Yacht Club located at Thunderbolt. The Savannah Yacht Club began in 1869 when it was organized as the Regatta Association of Chatham County. Josiah Tattnall, of Bonaventure plantation, served as the first Commodore of the association in 1870. John Screven was chosen as Vice Commodore and H. H. Woodbridge as Secretary under Tatnall. In 1871, the name was changed to the Regatta Association of the State of Georgia, reflecting the greater membership and role of the association. The Regatta first held races at White Bluff and by 1877 its headquarters were located at Montgomery, a resort town south of Thunderbolt. [86]

On 7 June 1876 the Regatta Association of the State of Georgia was reorganized as the Savannah Yacht Club, which was incorporated on 17 July 1882. The club built a new clubhouse on the Wilmington River in the 1880s, north of Thunderbolt's present business district (see Figure 6). The new club was a complex of several frame buildings connected by paths and boardwalks over the marshes (see Map 8). The main clubhouse was two stories crowned by an open cupola (see Figure 7). On the west façade, the entrance was flanked by two tower-like wings. The east side of the building opened onto the river with a two-story covered pavilion (see Figure 8). Pedrick's Pavilion, as it was called, provided the club members with a place to dock their yachts and gain access to the river. In 1886, twenty-four yachts were registered at the club in Thunderbolt. The pavilion was connected to the boathouse by boardwalks. By 1898, the club had added a bowling alley, and club facilities included billiards, shuffleboard, and an indoor marble swimming pool built at the expense of several thousand dollars. Several one story frame buildings were located northwest of the main clubhouse including stables, storage and a dwelling for the club's superintendent (see Maps 8 and 9, Figures 9 and 10). [87]

The entrance of the Savannah Yacht Club was impressive, with a long landscaped walk that began at the property's

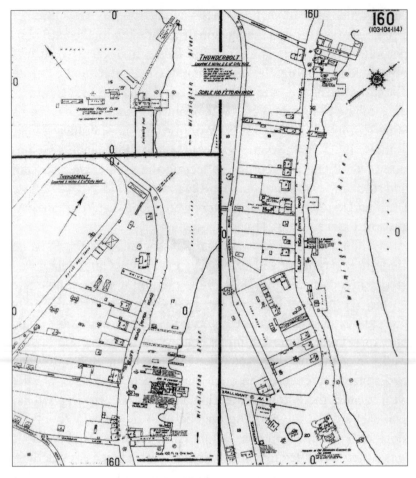

Map 9: Thunderbolt, Georgia, 1916
New York: Sanborn Map & Publishing Company, Ltd., 1916

entrance marked by an elaborate iron gate (see Figure 11). Visitors walked down the shell paved drive to the main clubhouse where they were greeted by a small fountain with a sculpture of a crane spouting water (see Figure 7).

Benches were placed along the bluff providing breathtaking views of the river to visitors (see Figure 12). A separate pool or pond adjacent to the clubhouse was built between 1898 and 1916, and was separated from the river by an embankment

SAVANNAH, GA. Savannah Yacht Club, Thunderbolt.

Figure 8: Benches along the bluff at the Savannah Yacht Club
Georgia Historical Society Postcard Collection VM 1361 PC, Box 8
Georgia Historical Society, Savannah, Georgia

Figure 9: Bathing Pool and Superintendent's House, Savannah Yacht Club
"Savannah Yacht Club." (Savannah: Braid & Hutton, 1905).
Georgia Historical Society, Savannah, Georgia

Figure 10: Keeper's Cottage, Savannah Yacht Club
Sutlive, W. G. "Savannah Yacht Club." *Outing, the Magazine of Amateur
Sport and Pastime Vol. XXXIII No. 5* (February 1899), 460.

Figure 11: Entrance Gate to the Savannah Yacht Club
Sutlive, W. G. "Savannah Yacht Club." *Outing, the Magazine of Amateur
Sport and Pastime Vol. XXXIII No. 5* (February 1899), 458.

Figure 12: River from the Savannah Yacht Club with Pool and Gazebo in Foreground
Georgia Historical Society Postcard Collection VM 1361 PC, Box 8
Georgia Historical Society, Savannah, Georgia

(see Map 9). Fish were kept in the pool to be cooked fresh in the club restaurant. Access to the club was aided by streetcars, which ran regularly from Savannah to Thunderbolt.[88]

The Savannah Yacht Club included among its membership the elite yachting class of Georgia, New York, Maryland, Pennsylvania, South Carolina and New Jersey, in addition to the local members from Thunderbolt and nearby Savannah. Local members included many of the most prominent in Savannah at that time, such as George J. Baldwin, Julian Schley and John Screven, Jr. Notable visitors to the club included President McKinley, Secretary of War Russell A. Alger, Congressmen William Jennings Bryan and several Georgia Governors. In 1889, the club's annual dues were $10.00, not exactly small change at the time. Annual regattas were held at the club, usually during the month of May. In 1893 the *Ocean Queen* triumphed over the *Eldiva* in the Fourth of July Regatta (see Figure 13). Motor boat races were also held along the river during the early 20th century (see Figures 14 and 15).[89]

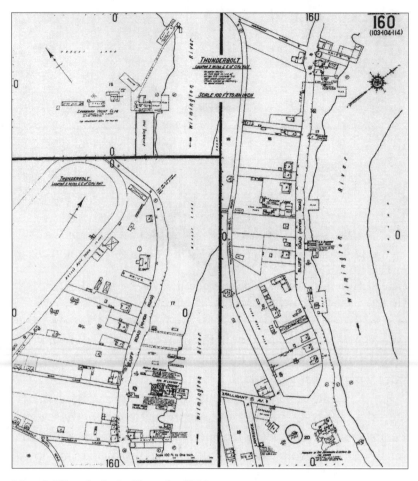

Map 9: Thunderbolt, Georgia, 1916
New York: Sanborn Map & Publishing Company, Ltd., 1916.

By 1915, the Yacht Club had become inactive. It was not until 1936 that the club was reorganized, at which time it was relocated to its present home on Wilmington Island, southeast of Thunderbolt on the opposite side of the Wilmington River (see Map 1). In 1923, the club property was sold to the Alee Temple of the Shrine and was referred to for many years as the Shrine Club. In 1944, the Shrine Club sold the property to James N. Lilley for $35,000. Lilley, the owner and proprietor of the Plaza

Figure 13: Boat Races, Savannah Yacht Club
Georgia Historical Society Photograph Collection VM 1361 PH, Box 27,
Folder 8, Item 5190
Georgia Historical Society, Savannah, Georgia

Restaurant on Broughton Street in downtown Savannah, developed the property as an entertainment center. His early plans, as recounted in the newspapers at the time, included a nightclub and a drive-in restaurant, a feature very popular at that time. By the time Lilley had bought the property, the owners had filled in the lowland marshes between the river and the road and the large pool. The unique frame clubhouse, with its cupola, was later lost to fire.[90]

Streetcars in Thunderbolt

On 20 December 1866, the Georgia State Legislature passed an act granting a twenty-year charter to the Savannah, Skidaway and Seaboard Railroad Company, commonly referred to as SS & S, to build and operate a railroad running from the City of Savannah to outlying communities. Included in the plan were the Isle of Hope, Skidaway Island, Montgomery, White Bluff, Thunderbolt and Green Island. The company was orga-

Figure 14: Motor Boat Racing, Thunderbolt
Georgia Historical Society Postcard Collection VM 1361 PC, Box 8
Georgia Historical Society, Savannah, Georgia

Figure 15: Motor Boat Racing, Thunderbolt, 23 March 1935
Cordray-Foltz Collection VM 1360 PH, Box 26, Folder 22, Item 1
Georgia Historical Society, Savannah, Georgia

Figure 16: Thunderbolt Streetcar
Georgia Historical Society Photograph Collection VM 1361 PH, Box 17,
Folder 11, Item 3554
Georgia Historical Society, Savannah, Georgia

nized with an initial capital stock of $100,000 with an option to increase stock to $200,000. By 1868, enough stock had been sold to fund the construction of the lines. Shortly after construction of the SS & S, the Savannah and Thunderbolt Railroad Company, otherwise known as the S & T, was incorporated in December of 1871. The S & T planned to leave Savannah from Abercorn Street and go to Thunderbolt, Beaulieau and Montgomery. Before construction of the S & T was completed, it united with the SS & S in February of 1874.[91]

During the 1880s, Alexander M. Barbee was the conductor running the regular route from the City Exchange on Bay Street in downtown Savannah out to Thunderbolt. Barbee later became the conductor of the Isle of Hope line, where he eventually moved and started the world famous Barbee's Terrapin Farm.[92]

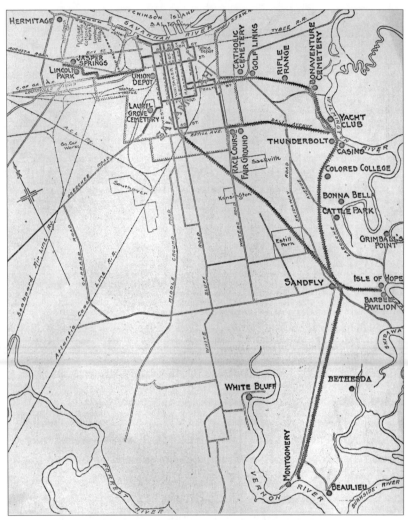

Map 10: "Map of Savannah Electric Company Lines"
Vertical File: Industry-Savannah-Savannah Electric & Power Company
Georgia Historical Society, Savannah, Georgia

The Coastline Railroad improved the streetcar lines in 1887, upgrading the lines going to Thunderbolt from horse to steam power. At this time the roundtrip fare from Savannah to Thunderbolt was twenty-five cents. Despite the fact that the town's official name was Warsaw at this time, the trolley cars were all labeled with "Thunderbolt," indicating Thunderbolt's enduring name and legend (see Figure 16). In 1897, the Coastline Railroad also departed from East Broad Street to go out to Thunderbolt.[93]

The Savannah Electric Company, which was incorporated on 27 December 1901, purchased the Savannah, Thunderbolt and Isle of Hope Railroad on 15 January 1902. At the same time, the company bought the City & Suburban Railway, the Savannah & Isle of Hope Railway and the Edison Electric Illuminating Company of Savannah. On 28 October 1921, the Savannah Electric Company merged with the Savannah Power Company to become the Savannah Electric & Power Company. Savannah Electric & Power maintained the streetcars to promote their interests in the outlying areas (see Map 10).[94]

As automobiles became more prevalent and popular in the United States and in the Savannah area the use of streetcars greatly declined until the last streetcar run from Savannah to Thunderbolt took place on 21 August 1946. Louise Johnson still remembers when residents could catch the streetcar into Savannah to shop. She would board the streetcar at Byrd's Corner, near the intersection of River Drive and Victory Drive, and paid five cents each way during the 1940s. When Johnson moved to Thunderbolt in 1942, Shell Road was still paved with oyster shells from Skidaway Road to the river front, "It was beautiful…if you looked out at night, the shell with the moon shining, it would glitter just like glass."[95] When they paved the road, over the oyster shells, the character of the neighborhood was somewhat changed.[96]

The history of the streetcars in Thunderbolt is intricately linked to that of Thunderbolt's resort activities. The Casino at

Thunderbolt and many of the outdoor amusements were developed to increase patronage on the streetcar lines. The streetcars were used the most on the weekends when Savannahians would venture out to Thunderbolt, Isle of Hope and Montgomery to go picnicking, boating, fishing, swimming, or to the Casino for music, dancing, and games. The streetcars also helped the development of suburban areas around Savannah, making previously remote areas more accessible. Locals in Thunderbolt could easily go into Savannah to shop and carry their packages and groceries home on the trolley.[97]

Thunderbolt Casino & Amusement Park

The Casino at Thunderbolt was built in 1895 by the Savannah Electric Company to increase patronage on their streetcar lines to Thunderbolt. The tracks ran right up to the Casino (see Figure 17), a large three-story frame building with expansive porches supported by white wood columns on all sides. The porches and balconies provided shade in the summer and views in all directions, of the river, marshes and amusement park. There

Figure 17: Streetcar Tracks and Thunderbolt Casino
Savannah Electric and Power Albums Collection VM 1381, Album 4.
Georgia Historical Society, Savannah, Georgia

Figure 18: Eastern Façade of the Casino at Thunderbolt
Georgia Historical Society Postcard Collection VM 1361 PC, Box 8
Georgia Historical Society, Savannah, Georgia

Figure 19: Southern Façade of the Casino at Thunderbolt
Georgia Historical Society Postcard Collection VM 1361 PC, Box 8
Georgia Historical Society, Savannah, Georgia

were two large pavilions on the north and south ends of the Casino. Broad staircases led to the main entrance, facing the bluff (see Figures 18 and 19).[98]

Figure 20: Thunderbolt Casino & Duck Pond
Georgia Historical Society Postcard Collection VM 1361 PC, Box 8
Georgia Historical Society, Savannah, Georgia

A pamphlet advertising the Casino could not have made it sound more enticing:

> *To him who is on pleasure bent, the Casino and Park at Thunderbolt offer everything to be wished for. The Casino building is large, well constructed and convenient, with spacious airy piazzas, a roomy and well ventilated auditorium, lighted by electricity, and cooled by electric fans, with a fine dancing floor, handsome stage and furnishings and the best orchestra in the county. Here is presented in the amusement season, vaudeville, comedy, minstrels, and comic opera. Dancing and moving pictures are furnished free for the pleasure of those who visit the resort.[99]*

The Casino was one of the first establishments in the Savannah area to show movies. Ernest F. Schmitt, a long-time

Feeding the Ducks, Thunderbolt. Savannah, Ga.

Figure 21: Duck Pond
Georgia Historical Society Postcard Collection VM 1361 PC, Box 8
Georgia Historical Society, Savannah, Georgia

---

employee of the Savannah Electric Company, ran the projector. The above description emphasizes that the Casino was built not only to increase business on the streetcar lines but to promote the popularity of electricity, with movies, lights, and fans all running on electricity.[100]

The grounds around the Casino were as exciting as the actual Casino facility. Built on parts of the Confederate battery, the site boasted two bandstands for concerts and dancing. One bandstand extended over the bluff onto a pier jutting over the Wilmington River. The second bandstand was a circular gazebo in the center of a large round duck pond west of the Casino. As at the Savannah Yacht Club, wood and cast iron benches lined the bluff overlooking the river (see Figures 20, 21, and 22).[101]

The Casino grounds included an amusement park which further promoted the interests of the electric company with electrical rides and games including a merry-go-ride and miniature roller coaster (see Map 9 for location of the carousel to the north-

Along the River Front at the Casino,
Thunderbolt, near Savannah, Ga.

Figure 22: Benches along the Thunderbolt Bluff
Georgia Historical Society Postcard Collection VM 1361 PC, Box 8
Georgia Historical Society, Savannah, Georgia

west of the Casino). Additional entertainments included a thirty-acre zoo and a beer garden. In one post card image of the Casino, tightrope walkers are performing on a rope set up over the duck pond at almost twice the height of the Casino building (see Figure 23).[102]

Once again the electric company's advertising pamphlet describes the resort and wonders that were once at Thunderbolt:

> *The grounds are large, beautifully laid out and*
> *well kept. On Sunday afternoons and evenings*
> *there are concerts by orchestra or band. The shady*
> *piazzas of the Casino are always well crowded on*
> *Sunday afternoons with people who go out to en-*
> *joy the cooling breezes and charming scenery, and*
> *the view of the river, with numerous craft of all*
> *kinds passing up and down, is a very pretty sight.*
> *The complete and extensive amusement park of*
> *the Electric Park Amusement Co. is provided with*

Figure 23: Tightrope Performers at Thunderbolt Casino
Georgia Historical Society Postcard Collection VM 1361 PC, Box 8
Georgia Historical Society, Savannah, Georgia

> *everything usually found at a first-class resort, the*
> *list including: a Tobagan [sic] Slide, Mystic Maze,*
> *Carousal, Circle Swing, Miniature Railway, Shoot-*
> *ing Gallery, Box Ball Alley, Etc...*[103]

The Casino enjoyed immense popularity during the late 19th century and early 20th century. As automobiles became wide spread, use of the streetcar lines decreased and Savannahians began to travel outside of the immediate area for vacations. By the 1920s the Casino had become run down and neglected (see Figures 24 and 25).

In 1930, Michael M. May bought the Casino after it had already changed hands several times. May renovated the property, hoping to revitalize it as a resort destination for dining, dancing and golf under the new name of "May Linx." The renovation

Figure 24: Thunderbolt Casino
Georgia Historical Society Photograph Collection VM 1361 PH, Box 17,
Folder 11, Item 6047
Georgia Historical Society, Savannah, Georgia

cost $60,000 and included adding an eighteen-hole miniature golf course, an archery gallery, and other sports. The golf course was designed by Arthur F. Comer, of Savannah, and was constructed by D. H. Wall, a Savannah landscape architect. The course utilized some of the old earthwork mounds from the Confederate battery as hazards and a "Confederate cannon" was placed on one of the novelty holes, with the object to get the golf ball into the mouth of the cannon (see Figure 26).[104]

On 2 November 1930, only two months after reopening, the Casino was completely destroyed by fire. The fire started in the basement and spread quickly in the heart pine building. The fire gutted the inside and an explosion in the basement caused flaming embers to fly through the night. All that was left when the fire was put out were the foundation pillars.[105]

Figure 25: Benches along the Thunderbolt Bluff
Georgia Historical Society Photograph Collection VM 1361 PH, Box 17,
Folder 11, Item 6046
Georgia Historical Society, Savannah, Georgia

Bannon Lodge

Bannon Lodge, the world famous restaurant, was started by Mrs. A. M. Bannon in 1875 in a small square building on her property adjacent to the Bannon House on River Drive. The streetcar line passed in front of the Bannon Lodge and as Thunderbolt became more popular as a resort destination, so did the popularity of Mrs. Bannon's famous she-crab soup, terrapin stew, and home baked rolls.[106]

As business expanded so did the lodge. Additions were made to the original structure and covered porches for outdoor eating surrounded the building (see Maps 7 and 9). The front had a large sheltered pavilion built around a large oak tree already on the property. The side deck had a small gazebo with a sign announcing "Bannon Lodge" to those approaching on the street or trolley (see Figure 16).[107]

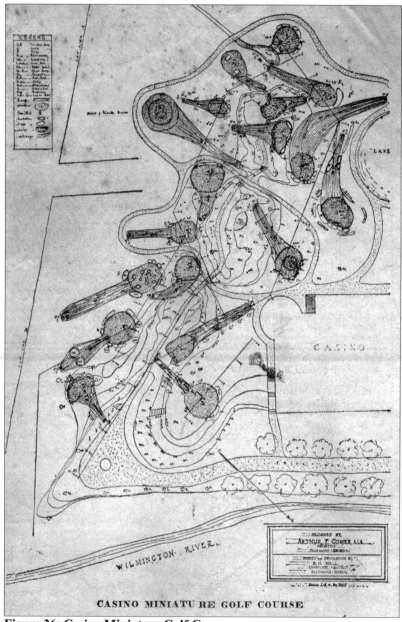

Figure 26: Casino Miniature Golf Course
"Work Starts on Casino Golf Course"
Walter C. Hartridge Collection MS 1349, Box 59, Folder 985
Georgia Historical Society, Savannah, Georgia

Bannon Lodge was one of the most famous restaurants on the south Atlantic coast and its visitors included several U.S. Presidents. When Mrs. Bannon died, her son James E. Bannon took over the operation until poor health forced him to close Bannon Lodge in 1936, ending a Thunderbolt legacy. In 1948, Mrs. Bannon's grandson, Harry P. Palmer, opened a new Bannon Lodge on Liberty Street in Savannah using the old recipes of his grandmother. However, the experience was not the same as eating along the river bluff with fresh seafood right off the docks and lacked the excitement of Thunderbolt at the turn of the century.[108]

In 1939, all the buildings of the Bannon Lodge, as it had grown over the years, were torn down leaving only the small original lodge. This structure was used as the first Catholic chapel in Thunderbolt and years later as a library.[109]

Bannon House, next door to the lodge, was one of the notable residences in Thunderbolt from the late 1880s. Built by Mrs. A. M. Bannon, the two-story red brick house boasted large columns and broad porches on the first and second floor, wrapping around the whole house, catching every breeze. The house sat on a large piece of property with two-hundred and fifty feet fronting the bluff and three-hundred feet deep. The grounds had pecan, fig, plum, grapefruit and palm trees. The home's yard was delineated by an ornamental iron fence. In 1943, the Bannon family sold the property to Louis G. Ambos and Henry Ambos, prominent Thunderbolt fishermen.[110]

The Ambos family purchased the Bannon House as an investment and in January of 1949 they leased the property to Lillian Pendleton Sinclair. Sinclair renovated the house into a rest home to accommodate twenty residents and named the establishment the Amelia Sinclair Hall for Elderly People (see Map 11).[111]

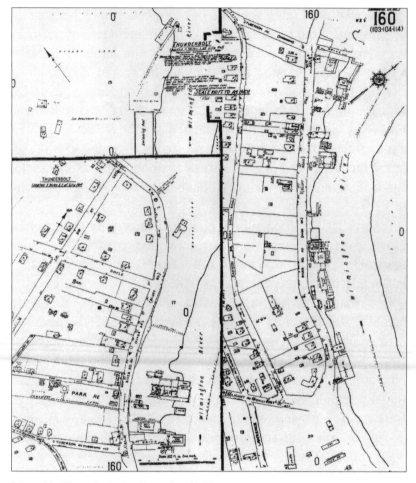

Map 11: Thunderbolt, Georgia, 1950
New York: Sanborn Map & Publishing Company, Ltd., 1950.

Doyle's Race Track

In 1868, Captain Marion Threadcraft, owner of Greenwich plantation and Park House Hotel, formed the Savannah Racing Club and built the horse racetrack at Thunderbolt, near the future site of the Savannah Yacht Club. The racetrack was complete with a wooden Grand Stand, two-story gambling house, bowling alley, shooting gallery, stables, and manager's house (see Maps 7 and 9). In 1880, Threadcraft sold the racetrack to Captain Michael J. Doyle. Doyle (1833-1907) was born in Ballyhunis, Mayo County, Ireland and came to the United States in 1849. In March of 1862, Doyle organized the Mitchell Volunteer Guards, Co. A, 47th Georgia Volunteer Infantry, and served as its captain. Following the war, he became a leading Republican in the State of Georgia, served as an alderman of Savannah, and was a grocer in Savannah.[112]

After Doyle bought the racetrack, horse and carriage races were held until about 1910 on the half mile track. In August of 1880, the park hosted the National Colored Baseball Association's First Annual Baseball Contest. Doyle's Race Track was considered one of the fastest horse tracks in the area. In addition to races, horse shows were held there, including the Chatham Hunt Club's Horse Show and Race Meet in April of 1909 (see Figure 27). The show included the following categories: single harness, gaited saddle, dealers' single harness, pair of matched, pony, gentlemen's roadster, best police horse, three-gaited saddle, single horse, and the hunter high jump. The Hussars races were between members of the Georgia Hussars, a volunteer militia unit of Savannah. The Chatham Hunt Club awarded blue, red, yellow and white ribbons for 1st, 2nd, 3rd, and 4th place respectively in each event.[113]

By 1918, the buildings were neglected and dilapidated. In 1945, Joseph A. Cesaroni and Michael J. Cesaroni, local fishermen, bought Doyle's Race Track for a housing development. Many residents of Thunderbolt still remember attending

Walkathons and Endurance Dances at the track before it was developed into housing (see Map 11).[114]

The Great Savannah Races

In 1908, 1910 and 1911, the City of Savannah hosted a
series of automobile races, a new phenomenon in the nation. At
the time, the Vanderbilt Cup Race was held on Long Island in
New York and the newly formed Automobile Club of America
hoped to compete with the Vanderbilt for racers and spectators
with a new, exciting race course in Savannah, Georgia.[115]

The first races were held on the 18th and 19th of March
1908. The preparation of the course resulted in the building and
improvement of many of Savannah's most famous drives, including Estill Avenue (present day Victory Drive), Skidaway Road
and White Bluff Road. The starting line for the Automobile Club
of America's Grand Prize Race was at Estill Avenue and Waters
Avenue. A Grand Stand for spectators and a Judges' Stand were
erected for viewing the start and finish of the races. The drivers
left the starting line and went west on Estill Avenue to White
Bluff Road, then south to Montgomery Crossroads, east passing
through Sand Fly Station on the way to the Isle of Hope. From
the Isle of Hope they went north to LaRoche Avenue and Skidaway
Road. The drivers then turned east driving to Thunderbolt and
finally back on Dale Avenue, returning to the Grand Stand at
Estill and Waters Avenues.[116]

The Savannah Races were promoted as safer than those
on Long Island. The City of Savannah set up thirteen guard sta-
tions along the racecourse to manage the crowds lined along the
sides and keep animals and humans from getting in the way of
the drivers during the race. Guard Position No. 9 was at Thunderbolt. The courses were also oiled three weeks before the events

Opposite: Figure 27: Chatham Hunt Club Program, 1909
Vertical File: Horses
Georgia Historical Society, Savannah, Georgia

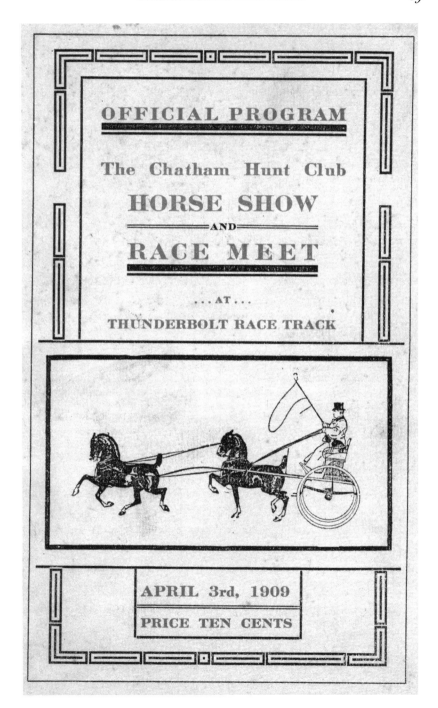

to reduce the dust on the dirt roads however this also increased the speed of the races, and therefore the dangers.[117]

The first Savannah races included the Southern High-Powered Cup (one-hundred and eighty miles), the Savannah Challenge Cup (three-hundred and sixty miles), and the Southern Runabout (one-hundred and eighty miles). Twenty cars, representing four nations, were entered in the races; Louis Wagner's Fiat won first place in the Grand Prize Race with a winning time of six hours, ten minutes, and thirty-one seconds. The races were a huge success, drawing more than 30,000 spectators. The automobile was still a novelty and Savannahians were impressed with the glamour and speed of the races.[118]

A few years earlier, the Mayor of Thunderbolt, William Aimar, bought a Model-T Ford. Aimar was ridiculed by some for buying into what was considered a dangerous fad and he had to apologize to local residents for driving around early in the morning blowing his horn.[119]

In November of 1908, a second series of races were held in Savannah. The biggest race was called the American Grand Prize Race and the winner received a gold trophy worth $5,000. The course was extended to include sections of Whitfield Avenue and Ferguson Avenue, taking drivers to Montgomery and Beaulieu, south of Savannah. The new course was enlarged from eighteen miles to twenty-five miles.[120]

The November races included the International Light Car Race and the Grand Prize Race, which was a total of four-hundred and two miles. The race drivers worked in teams and each team established a camp along the race course. The camps consisted of housing for the drivers, mechanics and personnel, as well as buildings for auto mechanics and storage of tires, gasoline and supplies. The Fiat team set up their camp at Doyle's Race Track in Thunderbolt.[121]

After 1908, the races did not include Thunderbolt. A new grandstand was erected in November 1910 on Waters Avenue near 46th Street. In November 1911, the Vanderbilt Cup was held in Savannah, but returned the following year to Long Island ending Savannah's auto racing experience.[122]

The races helped to give Thunderbolt exposure by drawing spectators and drivers in Savannah for the races to the river town. Unfortunately, the introduction of the automobile to mainstream society eventually contributed to Thunderbolt's decline as a resort by opening up new opportunities for travel outside of the Savannah area.

CHAPTER EIGHT
Thunderbolt in the Early Twentieth Century

Development and Growth of the Community

The beginning of the 20th century brought a period of growth and improvement to the community of Thunderbolt. Supported by the still popular Casino and opened up by the streetcar lines to Savannah, the population steadily grew. On 16 June 1921, a special resolution was passed officially changing the town name from Warsaw back to Thunderbolt.[123]

On 1 January 1902, Thunderbolt held its first mayoral election, ending the commission government in place since 1886. Lincoln Warren Nelson served as the first mayor, succeeded in 1904 by William W. Aimar, who served until 1920. (See Appendix B for a List of Thunderbolt Mayors). When the town was incorporated as Thunderbolt, Judge David S. Atkinson, town attorney, drew up a new town charter. The new government comprised a mayor and four aldermen supported by a town clerk, all elected on two-year terms. Open town meetings were held each month to discuss town business.[124]

Notable events in Thunderbolt's government include the election of Mrs. Laura E. Howe in 1945 as town clerk. Howe was the first woman elected to public office in Thunderbolt and held the position until her death in February of 1952. On 15 April 1949, Fred Rotureau presented his design for Thunderbolt's first official town flag at the Club Royal. The flag depicts an anchor and a thunderbolt representing the defining moments in

Thunderbolt's history. The anchor and the blue background reflect the importance of water throughout Thunderbolt's past.[125]

Thunderbolt began construction of the old Town Hall in 1912 on land along the bluff on River Drive sold to the town by the Wilharm family for $6,000 (see Map 9). The two-story building was finished in 1914 and shows classical influences in its design (see Figure 29). The first floor, made out of concrete, housed the town jail with four cells, a tool room, and a storeroom. Entrance to the jail was via a door on the southern side of the building, down the slope of the bluff. During high tide, prisoners had to be brought upstairs so that they would not drown as the waters rose.[126]

The second floor was actually on street level and the main entrance, with double doors and a transom, faced River Drive. Housing the court room, Mayor's office, committee room and bathroom, the frame building, though small, exhibited elements of Classical architecture giving it an air of importance. The front gabled building had a full pediment supported by an entablature with decorated frieze and large white wooden columns. The Classical design of the building stressed its governmental powers, like those in the U. S. Capitol, though on a much smaller scale.[127]

On 22 February 1932, Washington Day was held to observe the bicentennial of George Washington's birthday and a marble tablet and tree were planted by the children of Thunderbolt in front of the Town Hall on River Drive (see Figure 30).[128]

Improvements in the town included the installation of twenty-five street lamps on 8 June 1929 and the installation of a new water system in 1936. On 8 November 1935, the town voted on a $25,000 bond issue to expand the municipal water works. The issue was approved 127 to 7, allowing the town to accept $19,000 in Public Works Administration funds. This was the first bonded indebtedness in the town's history. The Works Progress Administration project involved the erection of a 100,000-gallon storage tank. The one-hundred foot tall tank provided good water pressure to the community for the first time.[129]

Figure 28: Bathing Houses and Docks along Thunderbolt Bluff
Georgia Historical Society Print Collection VM 1361 PR, Box 3, Folder 18
Georgia Historical Society, Savannah, Georgia

Figure 29: Thunderbolt Town Hall, built 1914
Georgia Historical Society Photograph Collection VM 1361 PH, Box 17,
Folder 11, Item 3559
Georgia Historical Society, Savannah, Georgia

Businesses in Thunderbolt in the early 1900s included restaurants and hotels catering to the resort visitors. Tuberson's Market and Savie's Store served the local clientele. Savie's was located on a pier with the store downstairs and the family's living quarters upstairs. Mulligan's Meat Market was operated by George Oliver Mulligan on Thunderbolt's bluff. The river town was dotted by docks and boats along its bluff (see Figures 28 and 31).[130]

Thunderbolt Yacht Basin

In May 1939, Asa G. Candler, Jr., son of the inventor of Coca-Cola, purchased the former Casino property, twenty-eight acres, from the estate of E. O'Bryan for $13,000. Candler, the Vice-President of Dunlap & Company, an insurance and bonding house in Atlanta, proposed building a yacht basin at Thunderbolt.[131]

After the Casino burned in 1930, the property had been vacant and the five and half acres of land and twenty-two and half acres of marsh were ready to be developed. The new basin, dedicated on 9 November 1939, was located on the intra-coastal water route from New York to Miami. At the time it was built, it was touted as the finest and largest basin of its kind along the Atlantic coast.[132]

The basin was constructed at a total cost of $75,000, including the purchase price of the property; R. J. Whalley & Company of Savannah won the construction contract. The marshes were dredged to create a basin five-hundred and ten feet long by two-hundred and ten feet wide. The basin was eight feet deep at low tide. A seventy-five foot floating dock was positioned near the bluff for yachts to pull up for gasing and servicing. Nine-foot floating dock slips could accommodate between sixty and seventy yachts at a time (see Figure 32).[133]

The seventy-foot wide entrance welcomed yachts traveling along the coast. A sixty-ton steel carriage railway and a twenty horse-power electric hoisting rig helped move boats in the basin

Figure 30: Washington Bicentennial, Thunderbolt
Cordray-Foltz Collection VM 1360 PH, Box 17, Folder 4, Item 2
Georgia Historical Society, Savannah, Georgia

Figure 31: Docks and Pavilion along Thunderbolt Bluff
Georgia Historical Society Print Collection VM 1361 PR, Box 3, Folder 18
Georgia Historical Society, Savannah, Georgia

Figure 32: Thunderbolt Yacht Basin
GHS Photograph Collection VM 1361 PH, Box 17, Folder 11, Item 3556
Georgia Historical Society, Savannah, Georgia

and remove them from the water for repairs. Large floodlights were installed to facilitate activity at night. The basin provided a midway point for boats to be reconditioned. Candler, a yachtsman himself for forty-two years, recognized the advantages of placing this type of facility in Thunderbolt where there were no freezes to damage the boats as in the North.

As the United States entered World War II, the strategic positioning of the Thunderbolt Yacht Basin was recognized. Within a one-hundred mile radius of Thunderbolt were sixteen inlets from the Atlantic Ocean. In November 1941, the United States government used the yacht basin as a shelter for mosquito boats. In 1942, Candler leased the basin to the government for use by the Savannah Army Air Base and the Army Air Force's "P" boats. The "P" boats were rescue vessels that could quickly get to downed airplanes offshore. Small torpedo boats were also reported stored at the basin. In 1944, the Third Air Force Staging Wing had a rescue boat station at Thunderbolt.[134]

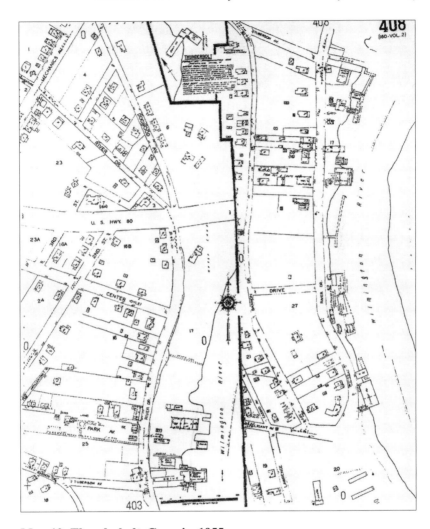

Map 12: Thunderbolt, Georgia, 1955
New York: Sanborn Map & Publishing Company, Ltd., 1955

After the war, the Georgia Air National Guard kept crash boats in the basin. By 1956, James N. Carter owned the Thunderbolt Yacht Basin. In 1965, the basin site was purchased by the Latex Corporation for $150,000. Later, the restaurant Tassey's Pier and the Thunderbolt Marina were located there.[135]

Natives of Thunderbolt remember climbing the water tank as children during World War II to pretend they were on the watch for enemies. No doubt, their imaginations were encouraged by the new boats housed in the basin.[136]

CHAPTER NINE
Thunderbolt the Fishing Village

Rebirth of a Community

The river played an even greater role in Thunderbolt's history in the 20th century as a connection to the coastal fishing grounds. Fishing had always been engaged in for pleasure and profit, but no one could predict the fishing explosion brought on by the growth of shrimping. As early as the 1850s, P. Gallagher had maintained a saltwater fish pond in Thunderbolt. He kept the pond stocked with Black Fish to supply his fish stall in City Market in Savannah. In 1860, George W. Lowden built an oyster cannery of tabby construction along Thunderbolt's bluff. The Lowden packing plant had an unloading room, cold storage room, raw room and steam room (see Map 9). There were several smaller oyster packing houses along the bluff, including that of Earl Toomer and Dewey Ambos. Lowden's plant was converted during World War One to can peaches. At the turn of the century, fishermen in Thunderbolt were successful but worked on a small scale, supplying Thunderbolt and Savannah primarily.[137]

Early businesses in Thunderbolt which catered to the fishermen included Adams Boat Works, B. T. Elmgren's boat works and machine shop and L. G. Ambos Boat Works, where boats were painted and repaired (see Map 9).[138]

The new century brought a rebirth of the community and a transition from a small resort dependent on the patronage of Savannahians and outsiders to a thriving town bringing in an in-

creasing income from the sea. There were three major events in
Thunderbolt during the 20th century that greatly impacted the fishing industry locally and nationally: the first was Paul Cannarella's
initial success shrimping out of Thunderbolt; the second was L.
P. Maggioni & Company's cannery and glass jar process; the third
was Trade Winds' development of pan-ready shrimp. Each event
increased the demand for shrimp and helped put Thunderbolt on
the map as an important seafood center. These events and the
efforts of numerous unnamed local fishermen created the special
community of Thunderbolt, a small fishing village with a unique
ethnic heritage.

Commercial Shrimping in Thunderbolt

Spurred on by the success of Paul Cannarella, commercial shrimping in Thunderbolt began full scale in the early 1920s;
by 1925 Thunderbolt was generating approximately 5,000,000
pounds of shrimp a year.[139]

Savannah was the major distribution point of the fishing
industry in the South and in 1925 the annual gross sale of fish,
oysters and shrimp leaving Savannah was over two million dollars. The shrimp export alone brought in $800,000 in revenue
through canned and fresh shrimp. In 1926, the city hosted the 6th
Annual Convention of the Southern Fisheries Association at the
old DeSoto Hotel on Bull Street on June 15th and 16th. Several
seafood companies in Thunderbolt were highlighted by the association for their success and importance to the local economy,
including L. P. Maggioni & Company, the Thunderbolt Fisheriers,
Cannarella Brothers, and the prawn fisheries of Thunderbolt.[140]

Several canneries were located along the bluff in Thunderbolt, canning oysters, terrapin and clam, but most importantly
shrimp. In 1925, there were eleven plants canning shrimp along
the Georgia coast, including those at Thunderbolt.[141]

The following is a list of several of the local families involved in Thunderbolt's shrimping industry, however there were

many more, including individuals who ran their own boats:

> Aliotta
> Louis G. Ambos & Henry Ambos
> J. S. Cafiero & Son
> Joseph Canas
> Paul and Vincent Cannarella
> Michael J. Cesaroni & Joseph P. Cesaroni
> Joe DeGracia
> Charles DeShocka
> Ricupero
> Earl J. Toomer Seafood Company

Many of the local fishermen were descendents of Italian, Portugese and even Scandinavian families with a history of fishing. For instance, Joseph Canas came to Georgia from Portugal at the age of fifteen and in the 1950s owned the shrimp trawlers *G. Philip Maggioni* and the *Santa Maria*. The attraction of fishermen to Thunderbolt contributed to the town's unique ethnic blend and high concentration of Italian-American families.[142]

The shrimp boats or trawlers would venture out as early as two or three o'clock in the morning and head out to Wassaw Sound. The trawlers would wait for the tide to be right for shrimping, when the water was low and the tide was on its way out. The storage pits below deck would be stocked with ice. "Otter trawls" or shrimp nets were towed by cables behind the trawlers. The nets were made by locals in Thunderbolt and a "net man" would hang around the docks in case their services were needed. In 1950, a net and crate manufacturing company had a plant in Thunderbolt to meet the demand. The nets were lowered to drag the floor of the ocean or sound, gathering shrimp and other sea life. When the nets were hauled in the shrimp and other seafood were packed in the ice to keep fresh while the nets were thrown back out. Local fishermen were catching mostly "Lake Shrimp." Lake Shrimp inhabited the saltwater ocean beds and inlets.[143]

The boats would return to Thunderbolt in the late afternoon to unload the day's catch. When the weather was cooler they could stay out overnight or even for several days because the ice would remain solid longer, maintaining the freshness of the shrimp in the storage pits. The returning trawlers unloaded their catch at the docks along Thunderbolt's bluff. Some of the docks would have a fish house on them to take in the incoming shrimp. After unloading, the boats would move out of the way to a holding deck where they would be repacked with ice and prepared for the next trip out. Some of the fishermen were part of a fleet bringing in shrimp to be processed at the canneries or shipped fresh all over the country. Several independent trawlers would sell their catch locally. Fishermen, as well as those who processed the shrimp, "were paid by piecework, for instance by the bucket or pound."[144]

When the shrimp came into the Thunderbolt docks they went through one of two processes, either canning or packing for shipment. The shrimp were scooped out of the trawlers in wire baskets, and after the ice was washed out, the baskets were weighed. At this point, with the shrimp no longer packed on ice, speed and efficiency became crucial to maintain the freshness of the seafood. The fresh shrimp for shipping were packed into large wooden boxes in alternating layers of shrimp and ice. When packed the boxes held one-hundred pounds of shrimp each and were loaded onto trucks, and later airplanes, to go all over the country. The majority of the shrimp were shipped north, most to Fulton Market in New York City where they were sold to wholesale seafood dealers. In the 1940s and 1950s, it cost about $5.00 to ship a one-hundred pound box to New York. In 1947, the Game and Fish Commission of Georgia reported that one-hundred pounds of shrimp were selling for approximately $45.00 wholesale.[145]

For shrimp that were going to be canned the process after weighing included heading the shrimp (removing the heads of

Figure 33: Heading the Shrimp
Cordray-Foltz Collection VM 1360 PH, Box 17, Folder 3, Item 12
Georgia Historical Society, Savannah, Georgia

Figure 34: Blanching the Shrimp
Cordray-Foltz Collection VM 1360 PH, Box 17, Folder 3, Item 13
Georgia Historical Society, Savannah, Georgia

the shrimp), peeling their shells, and blanching them in timed baths of steaming hot water (see Figures 33 and 34). The blanching process was not perfect and did not ensure even cooking among the shrimp. The blanching method was later improved by sending the shrimp through several timed baths, more evenly cooking all the shrimp. After blanching, the shrimp were put through a grader to sort them by size into small, medium, large or jumbo. They were then canned with either saltwater or a salt tablet in the can to ensure sea freshness for the customer (see Figure 35). Finally the cans were cooled, labeled and shipped out. During the 1920s, the *Savannah Morning News* published a series on Savannah's industries, including an issue on the fishing industry exclaiming Thunderbolt's success in sending shrimp as far as Los Angeles.[146]

During the 1930s and 1940s there were about one-hundred shrimp boats in Thunderbolt (see Figure 36). The boats were smaller than those used today and dragged only one net, about forty feet long. As refrigeration technology improved, the fishermen had the capability of storing the shrimp for longer periods of time while they continued to throw out their nets. Boats became much larger, operating more than one net at a time. The larger a catch the better their income since they were being paid by the pound for their hauls. The older smaller trawlers generally had a crew of two men while larger trawlers would take on a crew of at least three men.[147]

The shrimping season was initially from May to January, with the best months from September through December. Shrimp spawn in the ocean and then the new shrimp move into the saltwater inlets where they mature into full-grown shrimp. When the weather gets colder, the grown shrimp migrate back out into the ocean in search of warmer waters. As the demand for shrimp increased and refrigeration improved, Thunderbolt fishermen extended the shrimping season by broadening their fishing area. Prior to this most of the trawlers stayed between Charleston, South Carolina and St. Augustine, Florida. In order to extend the sea-

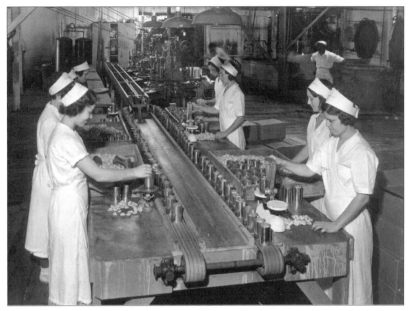

Figure 35: Canning the Shrimp
Cordray-Foltz Collection VM 1360 PH, Box 17, Folder 3, Item 15
Georgia Historical Society, Savannah, Georgia

Figure 36: Thunderbolt Shrimp Trawlers
GHS Photograph Collection VM 1361 PH, Box 17, Folder 11, Item 3558
Georgia Historical Society, Savannah, Georgia

son, fishermen began venturing further south into Florida waters near Key West.[148]

In 1950, the Thunderbolt fleets joined fishermen from South Carolina and Florida at new fishing grounds that had been discovered near the Dry Tortugas and Rebecca Shoals off of the Florida Keys. A brilliant run of the "Golden Brazilian" shrimp, or "pink gold" as the fishermen referred to them, was discovered in this area and shrimpers from all over came to join in the unprecedented harvest. Shrimpers brought in thirty to sixty boxes of shrimp in three days on an average. Each box was equal to one-hundred bushels or 5,000 pounds of shrimp. Normal hauls at this time were seventeen to twenty boxes for a whole week. The extension of the fishing area extended the season well past January.[149]

By 1974, when the industry peaked, Thunderbolt had one-hundred and fifty trawlers at its docks. When the boats came in at the end of the season, the break was used to make any necessary repairs to the trawlers, paint the boats, repair the nets for the next season, and catch up on much needed rest.[150]

During World War II, most of the Thunderbolt fishermen belonged to the Coast Guard Auxiliary and performed double duty by patrolling the coastal waters for enemy submarine activity. It was during this that the trawler *Norge* disappeared.[151]

The Cannarella Fleet

The Cannarella family has been involved in the fishing business in Savannah since the 1800s. A native of Sicily, Italy, Joseph Cannarella's (1852-1920) children included Paul and Vincent. One of his daughters married Antonio Cannarella Mathews, Sr. who was the largest seafood dealer in the City of Savannah at one time. Paul and Vincent came to Savannah from New York circa 1915-1920 and opened a booth in City Market selling seafood. The two later moved to Fernandina, Florida and became involved in the shrimping industry with the Versaggi family.[152]

In Fernandina, Paul bought his own fleet of shrimp boats and began shrimping off the Florida coast. He only stayed about one and a half years. In 1923 he conducted a survey of the inland waters and coastal offshore waters in the area of Tybee Island to determine if he could move his fleet into Georgia. The survey was conducted at the wrong time of year, giving Paul poor results so he returned to Fernandina. In 1924, John Hardee of Fernandina made a second survey with his fleet in the spring and discovered a large run of shrimp off the Georgia coast.[153]

Encouraged, Paul returned to Georgia in 1925 and approached Louis G. Ambos of Thunderbolt about renting land along the Thunderbolt bluff as a base for his shrimp fleet. In 1949, Ambos told the story to a Savannah reporter:

A fellow named Paul Cannarella came up from Fernandina around 1925. Wanted to rent a 50 foot front on the river from me to run a shrimp house-you know, boil them up in a pot and sell them. I didn't think too much of the idea, although individual fishermen had done the same thing at home for their own use for years, of course. But I let him have the place he wanted. Charged him $8 a month, I remember and my conscience hurt me a little bit at that. But, you know, it wasn't long till folks were standing in line to carry off his boiled shrimp.[154]

The streetcar ran in front of Cannarella's dock, which guaranteed a steady flow of customers coming in from Savannah for boiled shrimp on Sundays. During the week, Cannarella packed his shrimp for shipment to Fulton Market, receiving about 60 cents to $1.00 a bushel wholesale.[155]

With Cannarella's success, local fishermen started shrimping out of Thunderbolt and the new industry quickly grew bringing a new period of prosperity to the small community and giving birth to Thunderbolt, the fishing village.

L. P. Maggioni & Company, Plant No. 4

Lewis Paul Maggioni was originally from Monza in the Treviglio province of Italy. After running away from home, Maggioni became a cabin boy and ended up on a ship damaged by a hurricane in the Gulf of Mexico. He settled on the Gulf Coast and married Natalie, a native of Switzerland. In 1870, Maggioni and his wife moved to Savannah and opened a general store on the southwest corner of Bull Street and Gordon Street. From this small store, L. P. Maggioni & Company grew and expanded into the fresh fish business. L. P. Maggioni died in 1897; his son, Gilbert Philip Maggioni, took over the family business.[156]

Under G. P. Maggioni, the company continued to grow and started shipping fresh fish and oysters. With increased demand for seafood, G. P. Maggioni began experimenting with canning seafood; the company evolved into five canneries by the 1920s. The largest cannery was at Ladies Island, which had facilities to steam 3,000 bushels of oysters for canning under the *Daufuski* brand name. Maggioni became the largest supplier of cove oysters in the United States. Oyster production peaked between 1930 and 1935, as shrimp production was steadily increasing.[157]

G. P. Maggioni opened Plant No. 4 at Thunderbolt for canning shrimp. At Thunderbolt, L. P. Maggioni & Company had been the first to use a power trawler, circa 1910, while Paul Cannarella was the first to operate a power drawn net. Maggioni had their own fleet of trawlers and oyster vessels to supply them with the seafood for their canneries. By 1950, when the company celebrated its eightieth year, they had at least twenty-five hundred employees spread among their plants and fleets in Thunderbolt, Brunswick, Fernandina, St. Augustine, and South Carolina. Begun in the 1940s, the South Carolina plant canned vegetables, primarily tomatoes and okra. Maggioni products were shipped all over the country and had a healthy national market (see Figure 37).[158]

After G. P. Maggioni died in 1935, L. P. Maggioni &

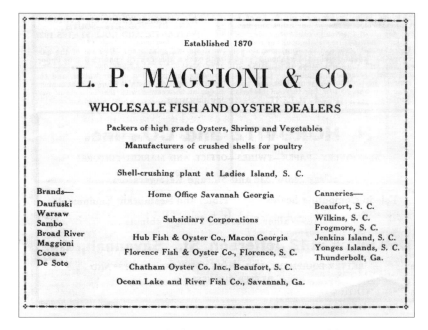

Figure 37: L. P. Maggioni & Company, Advertisement 1926
The Fish and Oyster Reporter (May 1926), 25
Vertical File: Fish and Shellfish
Georgia Historical Society, Savannah, Georgia

Company was run by family members. By 1950, the company was a partnership between J. O. Maggioni, L. Paul Maggioni, and J. C. Cafiero. In the 1960s, Paul Maggioni ran a retail market on Bay Street in Savannah, supplying the local market with seafood.[159]

Maggioni Seafood Plant No. 4, established in 1928 in Thunderbolt, was most notable for its support of the shrimping industry and the introduction of canning shrimp in glass jars. L. P. Maggioni & Company was the first packer to "preserve boiled shrimp in a glass container in the United States." The Thunderbolt plant averaged 50,000 pounds of canned shrimp a day. The plant comprised several buildings along the Thunderbolt bluff with a pier extending over the river. There were separate facilities for peeling, cooking and canning (see Map 11 and Figure 38).[160]

The shrimp trawlers would unload the catch at the pier in the afternoon and the shrimp were stored in a large refrigerated room until they could be processed the next day. After the two-minute blanching process, described earlier, the shrimp were boiled and canned in glass jars. About three-hundred workers were employed at the Thunderbolt factory. Black workers headed the shrimp, while white women cleaned the shrimp for cooking and then canned the boiled shrimp and labeled the containers (see Figures 39 and 41). The jars were cooled to ensure a proper seal before they were packed for shipment (see Figure 40). During the Depression, the majority of the teenage girls of the local Thunderbolt families worked in the factory. One native of Thunderbolt's mother worked there as a teenager for fifteen cents an hour.[161]

L. P. Maggioni & Company's local impact was further felt in 1947 after the New York manufacturer of their oyster grabs, a device used to harvest the oysters, discontinued production. Maggioni made an arrangement with the blacksmith of Georgia State Industrial College to produce the new oyster grabs for the

Figure 38: L. P. Maggioni & Company, Plant No. 4, Thunderbolt
Cordray-Foltz Collection VM 1360 PH, Box 17, Folder 3, Item 9
Georgia Historical Society, Savannah, Georgia

Figure 39: Maggioni Employees Canning in Glass Jars
Cordray-Foltz Collection VM 1360 PH, Box 17, Folder 3, Item 6
Georgia Historical Society, Savannah, Georgia

Figure 40: Cooling & Packing the Jars
Cordray-Foltz Collection VM 1360 PH, Box 17, Folder 3, Item 17
Georgia Historical Society, Savannah, Georgia

company, demonstrating the continuing pleasant relationship between the fishing community of Thunderbolt and the college.[162]

The Ambos Family & Trade Winds

The seafood processing company Trade Winds brought about a revolutionary change in not only the seafood industry but the grocery business in 1948 with their development of frozen pan-ready shrimp. The partnership between Henry Ambos and William Mullis became almost instantly a nationally famous company.

Ambos came from a prominent fishing family in Thunderbolt. His father, Louis Getz Ambos was born on 20 February 1886 in Thunderbolt. After renting the river frontage that started the shrimping business in Thunderbolt to Paul Cannarella in 1925, L. G. Ambos was the first native of Thunderbolt to begin shrimping in 1927. His first two trawlers were the boats *Sweet Pickle* and *Lindbergh*. By 1949, Ambos owned a fleet of ten trawlers. Ambos, as well as other shrimpers like DeShocka, would sell his catch to seafood dealers in Savannah and City Market. Ambos had a marine railway to pull the boats out of the water and into his repair yard.[163]

Louis G. Ambos was very active in local politics in Thunderbolt, serving on town council for forty-years before retiring in 1956. In 1949, as part of the first Blessing of the Fleet, Ambos was honored as "Mr. Thunderbolt," Dean of the Fishermen. After his death in December 1966, the town honored his role as citizen and fishermen by dedicating the 1967 Blessing of the Fleet to him.[164]

William Mullis was a grocer in Savannah for many years and thought that housewives would purchase more shrimp if they required less preparation to cook. Mullis came up with the concept of pan-ready shrimp and approached Henry Ambos in 1948 with the idea. Together the two experimented with methods of preparation and batters, freezing them at their homes to see how they would hold up being frozen and then cooked.[165]

Figure 41: L. P. Maggioni & Company Canned Shrimp
Cordray-Foltz Collection VM 1360 PH, Box 17, Folder 3, Item 8
Georgia Historical Society, Savannah, Georgia

Once they were satisfied with the process, they prepared five pounds of frozen shrimp for Mullis to market in his Savannah grocery store. Mullis sold the samples to his friends who assured him it was a quality product. Mullis and Ambos prepared fifty more pounds and then one-hundred pounds. It was obvious they had a success on their hands and they began distributing to five Savannah grocery stores.[166]

Mullis and Ambos formed a partnership under the brand name of Trade Winds.[167] L. G. Ambos & Sons' fleet of trawlers supplied the fresh shrimp to be prepared and frozen. Within a year, Trade Winds was being distributed all over the east coast, especially to New York. As demand increased the shrimp supply was supplemented with shrimp from Mexico, Alabama, Louisiana, Texas and even California.[168]

Trade Winds opened their seafood packing plant on River Drive in Thunderbolt. The shrimp trawlers unloaded their catches at the dock and the shrimp began an assembly line process, during which they were washed, weighed, cleaned and split, leaving the popular fan tails on. The cleaned shrimp were then dipped in an egg batter and rolled in cracker meal. After being packed in retail boxes and weighed, they were wrapped in plastic film and frozen. By 1950, 35,000 boxes were produced each day and the Trade Winds line had grown to include scallops, perch and oysters.[169]

The frozen shrimp were pan-ready for the housewife to cook. Within two years, Trade Winds products and Thunderbolt shrimp were sold in all forty-eight states and Hawaii. The company brought what had been a luxury item to areas previously denied access to shrimp.[170]

With the fast growth of the business in its first two years, Trade Winds opened a second packing plant and increased its employees from two-hundred and fifty to four-hundred, making it an important source of local jobs. At this time Trade Winds was bringing in $5,000,000 a year.[171]

The development of the frozen pan-ready shrimp changed

the seafood industry, expanding the market drastically. The less expensive seafood products were carried in grocery stores, eliminating to a certain degree separate fish retailers and expanding the frozen prepared foods industry that is such a large part of our society today. Locally, Trade Winds encouraged shrimping and provided jobs for fishermen and factory workers, as well as making Thunderbolt well known as the home of Trade Winds.[172]

The Cesaroni Fleet

The Cesaroni Fleet was started by brothers Joseph Adrio Cesaroni and Michael John Cesaroni. In the mid-1920s or early 1930s, the Cesaroni Brothers came to Thunderbolt from Apalachicola, Florida to join in the new shrimping industry. After working for L. P. Maggioni & Company managing their Thunderbolt cannery, the Cesaronis saved enough money to buy their first boat. In the late 1930s, the *Angelina* was the first trawler of what would become the Cesaroni fleet. The Cesaronis had continued success and bought the old Doyle Race Track in 1948. They developed the land as a subdivision, Cesaroni Homes, and most of the houses were built in the 1950s (see Map 11).[173]

After his brother's death, Michael Cesaroni continued the family business and by 1956 M. J. Cesaroni Fish Company was operating out of both Thunderbolt and St. Augustine, Florida. Cesaroni's daughter, Joan Cesaroni-Counsil, described the preparation the shrimp underwent when they came off of her father's trawlers. When the shrimp were unloaded, black families would head the shrimp in a trough with a tin bottom. The trough had running water on either side which washed the removed shrimp heads back into the river. The "headers," as they were called, were paid by the bucket for their work. The shrimp were then washed and drained before being packed in the wooden boxes. The boxes were loaded into trailers which left at night, headed for Fulton Market in New York City. Cesaroni also packed whiting and flounder for shipment and had a fish house in Thunderbolt from which he sold wholesale.[174]

In June of 1966, a fire caused $30,000 worth of damages to the Cesaroni operation in Thunderbolt, destroying the packing plant, store room, boat repair shop and three of their shrimp boats.[175]

M. J. Cesaroni, Jr. helped his father with the seafood business and served as Mayor of Thunderbolt in the late 1970s and early 1980s. His sister, Joan, served as the first woman on the town council in the 1980s.

Thunderbolt's Italian Community

As Thunderbolt grew as a fishing village it attracted many Italian families whose ancestors had been fishermen. As a result, today Thunderbolt has a large community of Italian-Americans compared to the rest of the Savannah area.

The Savannah Italian Club was organized in the early 1950s to celebrate the heritage of the community. In the words of one club member the "purpose of our club is to uphold the dignity of the word 'Italian.'"[176] The club bought the Bona Bella Point property just north of Thunderbolt for their activities.[177]

In 1971, when Thunderbolt's Old Town Hall on River Drive was razed, the four Roman Tuscan columns were salvaged and donated by Hendrix Southern Salvage & Wrecking Company to the Savannah Italian Club. The club erected the columns at the entrance of a new park named Town Hall Park in honor of the historic building the columns came from. Porter Huggins Construction Company helped to place the eight-hundred pound columns in a foundation of eleven tons of concrete according to the design of one of the club's members.[178]

The entrance, which took two months to complete, preserves a remnant of Thunderbolt's history and serves as a symbol of the Italian-American's contribution to Thunderbolt during the 20th century:

> *Italians pioneered the shrimp and seafood business in Thunderbolt, we felt it is a fitting tribute to them.*[179]

The majority of the Italian families settling in the area came originally from the Italian provinces of Campagna, Calabria, Abruzzi and Sicily. The Cafiero family held the Italian Consulate post for the Port of Savannah for three generations beginning with Joseph M. Cafiero.[180]

The Blessing of the Fleet

The first Blessing of the Fleet at Thunderbolt was held in April of 1949 on Palm Sunday. The Blessing of the Fleet was a religious ceremony and festival celebrating the fishermen and preparing them for the new season. The religious aspect of the festival came from the Blessings in the Roman Ritual of the Catholic Church. The Catholic religion provided numerous blessings asking God to guide one through life. Special blessings for different occupations included the fishermen:[181]

> *The Tiller of the soil, the herdsman, the shepherd and the fisherman are the producers of wealth; and the prosperity—even the existence—of the human race depends upon the success of their labor.*[182]

Father John A. Morris, of the Church of the Nativity of Our Lord in Thunderbolt (see Appendix A), proposed the idea of holding a blessing for Thunderbolt's fishermen, the lifeblood of the community. Father Morris recognized that the fishermen were dependent upon the forces of nature for their safety and a successful fishing season.[183]

> *The seaman and fisherman of all men, lives close, depends most completely on the elements of God's creation. His life and his livelihood are almost inseparably tied to the fancies of wind and sea and rain and tide. He realizes more fully than others his own inability to resist the powers of*

*nature. He and his little ship are often at the mercy
of forces over which he has no control.*

*The seaman knows how puny are his ef-
forts when pitted against the might of the sea. So,
before venturing forth to the open sea for the year's
fishing, he first seeks the protection of God for his
ship and his crew.[184]*

During the first blessing, a mass was held at the Chapel
of the Nativity, after which a procession made its way to the Thunderbolt Yacht Basin, where local shrimp trawlers were waiting to
be blessed by Father Morris with holy water. After the boats had
been blessed, a memorial wreath was laid on the river to remember those who had died recently or lost their life while performing their duties. Starting in 1951, the religious service was held
as a field mass.[185]

The first Blessing drew about three-thousand spectators
and sixty boats. In addition to the mass and Catholic Blessing,
the Blessing of the Fleet was a chance for the town to celebrate
its success and display its pride. In preparation for the contest of
the prettiest boat, the trawlers were painted and decorated. The
event gave "shrimpers a feeling of pride in their work, and their
boats."[186]

From 1949 until 1955, the festival included a parade of
floats. During the first year a replica of a shrimp boat complete
with a net was built. The float was invited to participate in the
Glenville Tomato Festival, as well as the Hampton, South Carolina Watermelon Festival. Local teenagers competed for the honor
of King and Queen of the festival. The very first King and Queen,
J. J. Keatin, Jr. and Frieda Hill, were crowned on 9 April 1949 at
a Coronation Ball, held at the Club Royale.[187]

Eventually the Blessing of the Fleet with the field mass
died out until later revived as a seafood festival sponsored by the
Thunderbolt Men's Club and the Jaycees in the month of June.
The new festival lacked the religious aspect that the Blessing

was based on and became a four-day event. In 1976, Reuben Ware wrote a song about the activities of the Blessing of the Fleet simply called "Thunderbolt."[188]

Thunderbolt's Centennial, 1956

In 1956, Thunderbolt celebrated the centennial of the incorporation of the town as Warsaw in 1856. The festivities were introduced through the induction of *The Thunderbolt*, a local newspaper dedicated to announcing current local events, as well as providing a historical retrospective of the town.

The Centennial Program, led by general chairman Paul Wilkin, included a Coronation Ball, Street Dance, Midway Carnival, Parade, Boat Races, Church Pageant, and a Prize Drawing. The Coronation Ball was held on the first day of the ceremonies, March 1st, at the General Oglethorpe Hotel on Wilmington Island. Tickets for the ball were $1.00 a person. Sylvia Ann Wood and Marion "Pat" Howard were crowned Centennial Queen and King. The Carnival was set up on a Midway with booths by Mr. Smith, the Carnival Man, and lasted all weekend.[189]

On 3 March 1956, the Centennial Parade, led by Louis G. Ambos, parade marshal, formed at Daffin Park on Victory Drive. After marching into Thunderbolt on Victory Drive, the floats took Mechanics Avenue to Bannon Drive all the way to the yacht basin before marching down River Drive to the old Town Hall. The boat races were open to racing teams from the southeast area and emphasized the river's continuing connection to Thunderbolt.[190]

Prince Preston, U.S. Congressman from Georgia's First District, in which Thunderbolt is located, was the principal speaker on Saturday and on Sunday the "Pageant of the Churches" was held, depicting Thunderbolt's religious history from 1732 through 1956.[191]

CHAPTER TEN
African Americans in Thunderbolt

The seafood industry was a uniting force between the white and African American communities in Thunderbolt. Unlike many businesses during the early 20th century, shrimping was not as discriminatory towards African Americans. Though the less favorable jobs in the canning and seafood processing factories were still reserved for black workers, there were many black shrimpers operating out of Thunderbolt who owned their own boats. Fishing was a family business with fathers teaching their sons the profession at a very young age. "They provided a future for them,"[192] by passing on the skills and leaving their boats to their children.[193]

Several black families were involved in the fishing industry, including the Murrays, the Washingtons, the Halls, and the Thorpes. These fishermen worked both independently, selling their catch to wholesalers, and as suppliers to the Thunderbolt seafood plants.[194]

African American residents of Thunderbolt were very important to the processing plants, providing much of the labor for processing the shrimp. Mrs. Elizabeth Ward, a native of Thunderbolt, worked for several of the larger seafood companies in Thunderbolt throughout her life. Though she handled shrimp on a daily basis, she can still say today, "I love shrimp!"[195] During the 1930s, Ward worked in L. P. Maggioni & Company's Thunderbolt plant, heading, peeling and cleaning the shrimp to be canned. During the late 1940s and the 1950s, she worked for Trade Winds, the first producer of frozen breaded shrimp, and finally the Ambos Plantation. In all three jobs, Ward split the shrimp down the back, from neck to tail, and cleaned out the vein and sand.[196]

Shrimping was vital to all in Thunderbolt. The industry promoted cooperation and friendliness between residents, while supplying a healthy income. Myrtle Baulkmon remembers never having to buy seafood because friends of her family who were fishermen would give them all the fish and shrimp they desired. The decline of the shrimping industry in the 1980s and 1990s hurt the black community the same as it did the white residents, with many losing their trawlers. The loss of a self-supporting industry greatly changed the community and many residents today reflect on a lost era of innocence and friendliness.[197]

Louise Johnson moved to Thunderbolt in 1942 from Savannah. She was attracted by the quiet and safe qualities of Thunderbolt, which promised a better way of life and a family oriented environment in which to raise children. According to Johnson, "It was wonderful at that time…Everybody seemed like one big family, we didn't lock our doors when we went out."[198]

Though times have changed, most African American residents still cite the closeness of the community as its most important quality today. Neighbors keep in touch and rely on one another. The importance of community and cooperation is encouraged by the Thunderbolt Community Improvement Association. Formed over fifty years ago, the Association is open to all members of the community. The group, which is the only active organization of its kind in Thunderbolt, has evolved into a primarily black organization with only a few white members.[199]

The Association was set up to support the community through improvement projects, neighborhood meetings and education. Support of the area children is a top priority. The Association built the Nellie Johnson Memorial Park in a vacant lot on the corner of Cedar Street and Falligant Avenue. Named for "Aunt

Nellie," a local woman who was very active with neighborhood children, the park is owned by the Town of Thunderbolt but maintained by the Association. During the summer, the group supervises a lunch program in the park for local children. In addition to the neighborhood park, the group contributes to the appearance of Thunderbolt with an annual clean-up campaign in April and community beautification projects.[200]

At their monthly meetings, the Association invites local town council members, prospective candidates, and the police, providing a forum for them to reach Thunderbolt residents. The police advise the residents regarding safety issues and the Neighborhood Watch program. Additional contributions to the community include a current project with the Savannah Sand Gnats to promote community spirit with a "Thunderbolt Night" at Grayson Stadium; financial support of Savannah State University's annual scholarship fund; and an annual Christmas luncheon given by the Association for Town of Thunderbolt employees to recognize their hard work. The Association is a large part of the African American community in Thunderbolt, promoting interaction and family-like ties almost lost with the decline of shrimping. [201]

Since the decline of the industry, a distinction between the white and black communities has begun to re-emerge. For the most part, the two operate as separate sub-communities parallel to each other. The loss of a uniting profession discouraged interaction and today the local government acts as the link between the two communities.[202]

In November of 1970, Leroy Brown was the first African American member elected to the Thunderbolt Town Council. Brown ran an auto mechanics shop on Falligant Avenue and was Assistant Professor of Mechanical Engineering Technology at Savannah State University. Brown, who had lived in Thunderbolt for over forty years at the time of his election, broke the barrier into the local government for African Americans. Today the government is mixed with blacks serving side by side with white residents and community leaders on the town council, the zoning board, and in the town's administration. Mrs. Myrtice Lewis emphasizes the importance of the African American residents to the entire community of Thunderbolt: "I think we [black community] have always been an integral part of the Thunderbolt community and very proudly so."[203]

African American residents were not limited to the fishing industry during the mid-20th century. Though many worked in domestic service, as was the case in many cities and towns at the time, there were numerous black business owners operating confectionaries, beauty shops, auto shops, and other businesses. After working as a maid for Henry Ambos' mother, Louise Johnson started her own business, Louise's Sandwich Shop, in 1946 next door to her home on Shell Road. Her small confectionary served sandwiches and hot dinners. Until she closed in the 1970s, Johnson catered to "everybody, foreign, white and colored." Johnson stressed that though her business was black owned her clientele was not strictly African Americans.[204]

George Dixon and Mr. Simmons are examples of farmers who managed to make a living by tending small plots around town. Owners of vacant lots would allow them to clear the land and grow garden vegetables, including butterbeans, okra, sugar cane, corn, collard greens and tomatoes. Dixon would then sell his goods in Savannah at City Market and at stands along the side of the road.[205]

Savannah State University also provided employment and business opportunities to the African American community of Thunderbolt. Louise Johnson's customers included students from the college and her husband worked on the campus tending lawns and gardens.[206]

The college did play a supporting role to Thunderbolt and vice versa, however it was not an integral part of the community. The black communities of Thunderbolt and Savannah State revolved separately much the same way the black and white communities within Thunderbolt did. Myrtle Baulkmon, who moved to Thunderbolt in the 1950s from Bainbridge, Georgia to attend the college, explained that many of Thunderbolt's black residents believed that the college students and faculty considered themselves superior to the locals because they had more education. Baulkmon noticed this but felt more accepted by the local community because she operated a small beauty parlor with the help of her mother out of her Thunderbolt home. The beauty parlor gave her ties within the community outside of her schoolwork. The reason for the distinction between the two groups can also be attributed to the fact that most of the students attending the college during the first half of the 1900s were from out of town and with only a short stay in the area did not create a strong connection with Thunderbolt.[207]

For many who moved to the area for school and then stayed, attending the college often became a family tradition with children and grandchildren following suit. Baulkmon came to Thunderbolt only after her brothers had already graduated from Savannah State and returned to the area after serving in the military. Residents of Thunderbolt and college alumni have only positive things to say about the college. Though it did not play a huge role in Thunderbolt, it did encourage the higher education of area residents, promoted a greater appreciation of the black community among the white residents, and helped to support local black businesses. One white native remembers delivering newspapers as a boy, and thereby coming into greater contact with educated black persons, which changed his racial perceptions.[208]

Mrs. Myrtice Lewis, a resident of Thunderbolt, grew up on the college campus where her father owned and operated B. J. James Confectionary. Benjamin Joseph James had come from a small town in Georgia to study agriculture. While attending school he started a small confectionary business, selling small candies and nuts, to support himself through school. The business grew into a general store with almost anything one needed. By the time James graduated in 1932, the business was so successful he did not pursue any agricultural work and ran the business on the campus for over forty years. James' success is a good example of the college promoting area businesses, but his store located on and serving the campus demonstrates how the college was a community all its own, separate from Thunderbolt.[209]

While Lewis was studying social studies in the 1950s, the college ran a Laboratory School where prospective teachers could receive training in teaching children. Many Thunderbolt children attended this school from the first through sixth grades. This project is one of the ways in which the school and Thunderbolt's African American community could work together to the benefit of both.[210]

The Savannah Tribune, the historically black paper serving the greater Savannah area are from the late 19th century through the 20th century, often reported events in Thunderbolt's African American community. The Thunderbolt columns generally announced births, deaths, marriages, out-of-town visitors, movements of the residents and the activities of the local churches. The paper's attention to the churches stressed the importance of the church in the African American community. Thunderbolt's black community still revolves around the four sister churches: Central Missionary Baptist Church, College Park Baptist Church, Litway Baptist Church and Wilmington Baptist Church. Though Central and College Park are the only two churches physically located within Thunderbolt town limits, the four work together, sharing Thunderbolt's African American population, and are involved in all aspects of the community.[211]

Wilmington Baptist is the oldest of the four and was originally located on Wilmington Island. At present, Litway Baptist is the largest of the four congregations with about seven-hundred members. Litway Baptist was formed in 1879 on Whitemarsh Island when several members of the Thunderbolt and Whitemarsh Island communities sought letters of dismissal from the First African Baptist Church of Savannah in order to organize a prayer house more accessible to their communities. The letters were granted and the first structure, a "palmetto camp," was constructed of palmetto poles and palms woven together to create a shelter. Jasper Holmes was the first to be baptized by the church. Holmes had joined the congregation after helping construct the camp. Though it was originally across the Wilmington River from Thunderbolt, Litway Baptist has always drawn from Thunderbolt's population. In 1921, the church moved to Thunderbolt and built a new church building on Shell Road (the present church is the third structure at this site).[212]

The role of the sister churches in Thunderbolt's African American community is very important. The church is involved in every aspect of community life and the pastor is expected to serve not only as a spiritual advisor but also as a political and social leader. Traditionally in most African American communities, including Thunderbolt, the black minister plays a "more integral role than their [his] Caucasian counterparts."[213] The sister churches have and continue to be involved with the community in child care and education, scholarship, travel, social events, and civil rights.[214]

The African American community of Thunderbolt is an important aspect of Thunderbolt's history. Though in many areas, especially the seafood industry, the white and black communities share the same past, there are important distinctions between the two, mainly the influence of area churches and Savannah State University on the local residents and the ongoing participation and cooperation of the Thunderbolt Community Improvement Association.

CHAPTER ELEVEN
Thunderbolt Enters the 21ˢᵗ Century

Decline of Commercial Fishing

The decline of Thunderbolt's shrimping industry began in the 1970s when the shrimp supply began to collapse. By the 1980s, it was almost impossible for a local shrimper to pull in a profitable catch. Hauls dropped so drastically that it would take shrimpers one week to bring in what had previously been a normal catch for one day. In the 1990s, only a few fishermen still operated out of Thunderbolt.[215]

Reasons for the decline of the shrimp are mixed. Some blame it on pollution of the rivers, others on over-shrimping. The fast growth and success of the shrimping industry attracted a lot of outsiders who came to cash in on Thunderbolt's success. In addition to more trawlers in the area, the boats themselves got larger with more nets as technology improved. With so many boats all vying for the shrimp, fishermen did not wait for the shrimp to mature and spawn, causing a decline in the local shrimp population. Fishermen now check the size of the shrimp to prevent this. As the shrimping industry declined many local fishermen left to follow the catch, migrating to places like Brownsville, Texas, Patterson, Louisiana, and Florida.[216]

Those who remained in Thunderbolt turned to other sources of income; today the majority of Thunderbolt's residents are employed outside of the community. As a result, Thunderbolt is becoming more like a suburb of Savannah than an independent community (see Map 13 for current city limits).[217]

When Louis G. Ambos II and his twin brother, Henry F. Ambos, Jr., quit shrimping in 1988 it marked the end of the Ambos fishing legacy, as well as representing the end of the most important period in Thunderbolt's history. The Ambos brothers built a new marina on River Drive on property purchased by their grandfather, Louis G. Ambos, in 1903. They later sold the property for the development of condominiums.[218]

The Fishermen's Memorial

On 22 June 1996 the Fishermen's Memorial was dedicated by the Angler's Reef Fishing Club of Thunderbolt. Pat. M. Smith, a Thunderbolt native, came up with the concept of the memorial to honor those who "toil in the seafood industry." The memorial, dedicated to those in the seafood industry, is even more importantly a symbol of the town's "fading heritage," and the decline of local fishing.[219]

The memorial was erected on River Drive on land once owned by the Ambos family, who were instrumental in Thunderbolt's seafood industry. The project was funded by private donations and the sale of commemorative bricks. The two-year project resulted in a thirteen-foot mahogany cross mounted on top of a seventy inch by thirty inch brick foundation comprised of four-hundred bricks with the names of local families and fishermen. The monument is located between two of the large oak trees that grace the Thunderbolt bluff, the heart of the town since the 1730s.[220]

A New Architectural Landscape

The architectural landscape of Thunderbolt is undergoing a dramatic transition along the historic bluff. As the shrimp trawlers disappeared, the need for docks and marinas did as well, leaving a wide swath of valuable land open for redevelopment. A new industry has emerged in Thunderbolt, though the benefits go primarily to outside developers and investors. Condomini-

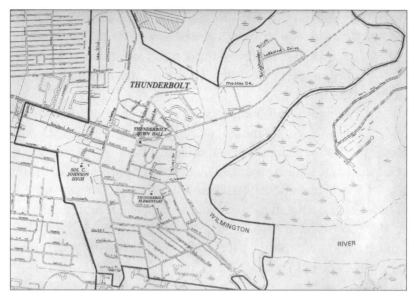

Map 13: Current Thunderbolt Town Limits
Thunderbolt Museum Society, Thunderbolt, Georgia

ums along the bluff are filling the high demand for summer living year round and attract residents from Savannah and outside the immediate area. The condominiums not only change the character and scale of the bluff, and the streetscape and views of the river, but introduce new residents to the community. In addition, to bringing in new owners, the concept of the condominium promotes their use as rental properties. A shift from resident owners to rental tenants can change the character and pride of a neighborhood.[221]

Thunderbolt Museum Society

The Thunderbolt Museum Society held its first meeting on 17 January 2001. The purpose of the Society is to preserve and promote the history of Thunderbolt. A new museum was recently opened in the vacated Town Hall on the corner of Mechanics Avenue and Victory Drive. The building was the old Thunderbolt School and was purchased by the town from the

Board of Education in 1967 for $37,500. The town remodeled the building over a four-month period at a cost of $25,000, relying on the help of Thunderbolt aldermen and town volunteers. The building housed the Town Hall until the present building was constructed in 2000-2001.[222]

The new Town Hall, located on River Drive, houses all of Thunderbolt's government including administration, the court room, the Police Department, the Department of Public Works and the Finance Department. The new building was paid for by a 1998 bond issue and cost $1.1 million. The 10,000 square foot building was designed by Rick Gilpin of G. B. Designs in Savannah and constructed by R. L. Construction of Thunderbolt. The front portico and columns recall the old Town Hall's Classical elements. The old Town Hall was located on the opposite side of River Drive but was moved in 1988. The old town jail was demolished and the site was filled in and sold. By moving the new Town Hall back to River Drive, the town has recaptured the importance of the bluff as the heart of Thunderbolt's business and government.[223]

Conclusion

When asked what they remember most about growing up in Thunderbolt, natives fondly speak of the river and the excitement along the docks, stating emphatically that Thunderbolt was a great place to be a child. The river continues to be the defining characteristic of the small community. It has guided the town through over two-hundred and fifty years of growth and development, providing Thunderbolt with the means to adapt to changing social, environmental and economical factors. The river will continue to chart Thunderbolt's future and tie the unique community to its rich past.

APPENDIX A
Thunderbolt Area Churches

Central Baptist Missionary Church

On Bannon Drive near Mechanics Avenue, a prayer house was erected by area blacks as a branch of the First African Baptist Church of Savannah. On 3 January 1900, the church split and formed an independent congregation under the name Central Baptist Church. Central Baptist is considered one of the four sister churches, which include Litway Baptist and Wilmington Baptist (outside of Thunderbolt's city limits), and College Park Baptist.[224]

Church of the Nativity of Our Lord

The Catholic Church of the Nativity of Our Lord is located on Mechanics Avenue at Victory Drive. It began in 1918, when Mrs. Nellie Dowling and Mrs. Rosalind Ward started Sunday School classes in the Glaiber home in Thunderbolt. In 1926, the classes were moved to the Elmgren home on Mechanics Avenue. From 1936 until 1942, a small mission chapel was held in the old Bannon Lodge on River Drive. In 1947, construction of the new two-story brick sanctuary on Mechanics Avenue began (present location). By October the church was ready for occupation and on 2 November 1947, the church was officially dedicated. In 1951, the Sisters of Mercy started a small school in the church.[225]

Saint Luke's Lutheran Church

Saint Luke's is located on Mechanics Avenue in Thunderbolt in a building that has been an important part of the community for over one-hundred years. The church sanctuary is the oldest still standing in Thunderbolt. In 1929, the property of the Union Church was transferred to the Lutheran pastors, C. A. Linn, H. J. Black and T. S. Brown, acting as Trustees for a Lutheran congregation yet to be organized in Thunderbolt. The old Union Church was repaired and remodeled, creating a chancel, choir, sacristy and bathrooms. The altar was a gift of the Lutheran Church of Birmingham, Alabama and had previously been in the Lutheran Church of the Ascension in Savannah. Saint Luke's Lutheran Church was organized with twelve charter members including the Ambos, Elmgren, Griffin, and Oetgen families. Saint Luke's Lutheran Church held their first services on 9 November 1930 with Pastor Alfred Shelley. Shelley served the congregation for fifteen years until his death in 1946. After his death in February, his home, adjacent to the church, was purchased as a parsonage for Saint Luke's. The Educational Hall, later named Rohde Memorial Building, was dedicated in 1935 for the Sunday School. In 1962, the congregation moved into a new sanctuary and remodeled the old church into a social hall, named in honor of Pastor Shelley. During renovations the cupola and bell, cross, and narthex were removed.[226]

Sunset Baptist Church

Sunset Baptist Church was organized in 1955 by a small group with the guidance of Reverend J. A. King. Reverend R. C. O'Berry served as the first pastor. In February of 1956, the church started construction of a church building on the south side of Sunset Boulevard in Sunset Park. In June, the congregation moved into the new frame structure.[227]

Thunderbolt Baptist Church

Located on Bannon Drive, the Thunderbolt Baptist Church was organized on 20 November 1951. Before dedicating their new church on 9 November 1952, church meetings were held in W. W. Hall's home and the Thunderbolt Town Hall. Reverend Richard D. Hinely was the first pastor, followed by S. J. Lawson in 1956.[228]

Thunderbolt Presbyterian Chapel

In 1912, those of the Presbyterian denomination worshipped in the "Little Red Chapel" on Falligant Avenue, built by Mayor William W. Aimar. In 1922, James N. Moore, of the First Presbyterian Church of Savannah, started a Sunday School in the old Union Church with about thirty-five students. The Thunderbolt Presbyterian Chapel was officially organized on 6 February 1923 with twenty-five charter members. The cornerstone for a chapel was laid on 29 March 1925 on Bannon Drive (see Map 11). Reverend Arthur Morrison Martin, served as their first pastor from 1928 until 1938. The chapel was originally a member of the Savannah Presbytery. In July of 1948, they left the Savannah Presbytery and became a chapel under Independent Presbyterian Church of Savannah.[229]

Union Church

On 6 April 1895 the Union Church of Warsaw was granted its original charter for a period of twenty years. Named for the official name of the town at the time, the church was commonly referred to as the Union Church of Thunderbolt. On 29 June 1903 the small frame building with a cupola, erected at a cost of $1,600, was dedicated. The building seated two-hundred and fifty people and was led by Reverend John S. Wilder when it started. Services were held one Sunday a month for those of the Methodist, Presbyterian and Baptist denominations. In 1929, the Trustees of the church passed a resolution to turn over the church building to a Lutheran congregation, which became Saint Luke's.[230]

Wesley Oaks Methodist Church

Wesley Oaks was named for the oak trees along Thunderbolt's bluff under which John Wesley preached to the colonial settlers and the Indians while he was in Georgia. It is the first church to be organized of those remaining today. In 1910, a group of Methodists that had been attending the Union Church decided to withdraw and establish their own church. The congregation purchased two lots on Dale Avenue (Victory Drive) on 10 May 1912. The first sanctuary was constructed of rough lumber with wooden benches. In 1915, a new frame church was erected. The church is located on Victory Drive at Mechanics Avenue, across from the Church of the Nativity. In 1948, the Falligant Home on Mechanics Avenue, adjacent to the church, was purchased as the church parsonage. In 1956, the church put the old sanctuary on a new basement, providing new Sunday School rooms, a Pastor's study and a utility room. Today the stuccoed building has a beautiful stained glass window over the main entrance.[231]

APPENDIX B
Thunderbolt's Government

"Thunderbolt Flag!"
Behold! Our Flag, a symbol
Of "Things Done" and not "Things Said,"
May it ever hold us steadfast
On the pathway we must tread
Like the anchor on it's bosom,
Set in purest, solid Gold,
May it ever be Symbolic
Of the Pride our duties hold.
May it fly throughout the Ages
And inspire men to their best,
May they gaze with joy upon it
And rise up to meet each Test."
-Mayor Paul E. Wilkin[232]

Former Mayors of Thunderbolt

Lincoln Warren Nelson	?-January 1904
William W. Aimar	January 1904-January 1920
E.O. Bryan	January 1920-July 1932
Samuel L. Byrd	July 1932-January 1946
Herbert Lee Wood, Sr.	January 1947-June 1950
Paul E. Wilkin	June 1950-January 1951
Herbert Lee Wood, Sr.	January 1951-June 1954
Arthur D. Gallagher	July 1954-January 1955
Frank T. Wall	January 1955-January 1957
Russell B. Pead	January 1957-January 1961
William E. Mullis, Jr.	February 1961-August 1962
Arthur D. Gallagher	August 1962-January 1963
B. Arthur Gilreath	January 1963-October 1970
Hal C. Lane	January 1970-October 1972
B. Arthur Gilreath	October 1972-October 1974
Hal C. Lane	January 1974-January 1978
Michael J. Cesaroni	January 1978-January 1981
James A. Petrea	January 1981-present

Endnotes

[1] *Thunderbolt Museum Society Scrapbook.*

[2] Workers of the Writers' Program of the Works Progress Administration of the State of Georgia, *Georgia: The WPA Guide to its Towns and Country-side* (University of South Carolina Press), 261; E. L. Shearouse, "Southern History," *The Thunderbolt Vol. 1 No. 3* (16 March 1956), 2; Roulhac Toledano, *The National Trust Guide to Savannah* (New York: John Wiley and Sons, Inc., 1997), 197; "Queries and Answers," *Georgia Historical Quarterly Vol. I No. 3,* p 275; Sylvia Wood, "The Naming of Thunderbolt," *The Thunderbolt Vol. 1 No. 1* (19 February 1956), p 3; William Harden, *A History of Savannah and South Georgia, Vol. 1* (Atlanta: Cherokee Publishing Company, 1969), 199; "Map of Thunderbolt, Georgia," (T.M. Reed, 1976).

[3] Harden, 199.

[4] "Queries and Answers," *Georgia Historical Quarterly Vol.I No. 3,* 275.

[5] "Map of Thunderbolt, Georgia"; Vin Whitson, "History of Thunder-bolt," "Thunderbolt, Georgia Centennial 1856-1956," (2-5 March 1956) Official Program, 22.

[6] John Gerar William DeBrahm, *History of the Province of Georgia with Maps of Original Surveys* (Wormsloe: MDCCCXLIX), 28.

[7] *Thunderbolt Vertical File*, Georgia Historical Society, Savannah, Georgia (hereafter referred to as GHS).

[8] Toledano, 197.

[9] Laura Palmer Bell, "A New Theory on the Plan of Savannah," *The Georgia Historical Quarterly Vol. 48 No. 2* (June 1964), 156; Thomas W. Hodlee and Howard A. Schretter, *The Atlas of Georgia* (Athens: The University of Georgia Press, 1986), 65.

[10] Preston Russell and Barbara Hines, *Savannah: A History of Her People Since 1733* (Savannah: Frederic C. Beil, Publishers, 1992), 14; Adelaide Wilson, *Historic and Picturesque Savannah* (Boston: Boston Photogravure Company, 1889), 19; Carl Solana Weeks, *The Road to Revolution in Colonial Georgia: Savannah in the Time of Peter Tondee* (Columbia: Summerhouse Press,

1997), 43; Whitson, 22.

[11] Toledano, 197.

[12] Harden, 199; Whitson, 22, 24.

[13] John Percival, the first Earl of Egmont, was one of the most important figures in the founding of the Colony of Georgia, behind General James Oglethorpe. While Oglethorpe accompanied the colonists to Georgia, Percival remained in England, offering advice and working with the Trustees in England. Percival served as the first President of the Trustees and attended the meetings regularly between 1732 and 1744, keeping a detailed journal of the Trustees meetings, which provide valuable insight into the establishment and development of the fledgling colony (Robert G. McPherson, ed., *The Journal of the Earl of Egmont: Abstracts of the Trustees Proceedings for Establishing the Colony of Georgia, 1732-1738* (Athens: The University of Georgia Press, 1962).

[14] Floyd, 3.

[15] McPherson, 23; M. H. & D. B. Floyd, "Thunderbolt," M. H. and D. B. Floyd Collection MS 1308, GHS, 6.

[16] Floyd, 3-4; McPherson, 24.

[17] McPherson, 29; Floyd, 6.

[18] "Roger Hugh Lacey, the First Grand Master of Masons in Georgia," *Alee Temple Fez* (August 1961), 4.

[19] E. Merton Coulter and Albert B. Saye, eds., *A List of the Early Settlers of Georgia*, (Athens: The University of Georgia Press, 1949), 81.

[20] Floyd, 5, 9; *Alee Temple Fez*, 4; McPherson, 215; Whitson, 22.

[21] *Alee Temple Fez*, 4; "Centennial Celebration is On," *The Thunderbolt Vol. 1 No. 2* (4 March 1956), 1.

[22] McPherson, 168; *Alee Temple Fez*, 4; Floyd, 13.

[23] Floyd, 15; *Alee Temple Fez*, 4.

[24] Weeks, 58; Floyd, 14, 18; Coulter and Saye, 64, 78.

[25] *Alee Temple Fez*, 4; Floyd, 5; Whitson, 22.

[26] McPherson, 308.

[27] Floyd, 7.

[28] James Etheridge Callaway, *The Early Settlement of Georgia* (Athens: The University of Georgia Press, 1948), 22-23.

[29] William Stephens served as Secretary of the Province of Georgia from 1737 to 1750 and as President of the Province of Georgia from 1741 until 1751. While in Georgia, he wrote to the Trustees in England, keeping them abreast of the current situation, as well as maintaining a detailed journal.

[30] Floyd, 7-8; Callaway, 22-23; McPherson, 237.

[31] Floyd, 14.

[32] Floyd 2, 22; Toledano, 197.

[33] E. Merton Coulter, ed., *The Journal of William Stephens, 1743-1745,*

Vol. 1 (Athens: The University of Georgia Press, 1958), 102.

[34] Floyd, 2, 23, 27.

[35] Harden, 199; Floyd, 22, 23, 27.

[36] Floyd, 30, 31.

[37] The name Bonaventure comes from "Buona Ventura," Italian for Good Fortune.

[38] Floyd, 27, 29, 32.

[39] Floyd, 33.

[40] Rabbi Saul Jacob Rubin, *Third to None, the Saga of Savannah Jewry, 1733-1983* (Savannah: The Congregation Mickve Israel, 1983), 29.

[41] Rubin, 29.

[42] Levi Sheftall was on the list of Tory sympathizers, however in 1785 an act of the General Assembly restored his citizenship, taking actions like the above into account.

[43] Weeks, 221; Rubin, 30, 35.

[44] Bonaventure Historic Society, *Bonaventure Cemetery, Savannah, Georgia, Index Section A-H* (Savannah: Bonaventure Historic Society, Inc., 2000), ix; Ron Freeman, *Savannah People, Places and Events* (Savannah: H. Ronald Freeman, 2000), 144; Margaret Wayt DeBolt, *Savannah: A Historical Portrait* (Virginia Beach: The Donning Company, Publishers, Inc., 1976), 58; Whitson, 22; Antoine O'Connor, "Map of Savannah, n.d.," Waring Maps Collection MS 1018 (hereafter referred to as MS 1018), Vol. 3, Plate 22, GHS; "Siege De Savanah, 1779," MS 1018, Vol. 3, Plate 24, GHS.

[45] Investigations have led historians to believe that the battle took place near the Savannah History Museum, which is located at the intersection of Martin Luther King, Jr. Boulevard and Louisville Road in Savannah, Georgia.

[46] Weeks, 223.

[47] Bonaventure Historic Society, ix; Weeks, 223; Rubin, 70-71.

[48] Bonaventure Historic Society, xi.

[49] Tattnall Street in Savannah and Tattnall County, Georgia were named in honor of Josiah Tattnall, Jr.

[50] Bonaventure Historic Society, xi.

[51] John McKinnon, "Plan of Savannah, c1800," MS 1018, Vol. 2, Plate 4, GHS.

[52] John McKinnon, "Liberty Island, 1823," MS 1018, Vol. 3, Plate 42, GHS; Whitson, 24; Mary Granger, ed., *Savannah River Plantations* (Savannah: Georgia Historical Society, 1947), 11; Savannah Unit, Federal Writers' Project, "Causton's Bluff, Deptford, Brewton Hill, Three Allied Plantations," *The Georgia Historical Quarterly Vol. 23 No. 1* (March 1939), 38.

[53] Granger, 208, 218, 409, 429.

[54] Bonaventure Historic Society, ix, x; DeBolt, 112.

[55] John McKinnon, "Liberty Island, 1823," MS 1018, Vol. 3, Plate 42,

GHS; Curtis Carroll Davis, "Dr. Caruthers Confronts the Bureaucrats," *The Georgia Historical Quarterly Vol. 56 No. 1* (Spring 1972), 111; Ann Stoddard, "Thunderbolt, 1973," (TMs, photocopy), Georgia Room, Bull Street Branch, Chatham-Effingham-Liberty Counties Library, Savannah, Georgia (hereafter referred to as Bull Street Library), 48.

[56] Stoddard, 37.

[57] Sylvia Wood, "The Naming of Thunderbolt," *The Thunderbolt Vol. 1 No.1* (19 February 1959), 3; Freeman, 188; Floyd, 3; "Queries and Answers," *The Georgia Historical Quarterly Vol. 1 No. 3*, 276.

[58] DeBolt, 43; Jim Miles, *Civil War Sites in Georgia* (Nashville: Rutledge Hill Press, 1996), 193.

[59] Roger W. Young, "Two Years at Fort Barstow, 1862-1864," *The Georgia Historical Quarterly Vol. 23 No. 3* (September 1939), 255-256.

[60] Claudia B. Lamas, "Fortification Survey of the Savannah River and Area Waterways, Savannah, Georgia, 1861-1865," (TMs, photocopy), Minis Room, Lane Library, Armstrong Atlantic State University, Savannah, Georgia, 11; Derek Smith, *Civil War Savannah* (Savannah: Frederic C. Beil, Publishers, Inc., 1997), 89.

[61] Smith, 89; Lamas, Map 8, Figures 4, 5; Whitson, 24; "The Capture of the U.S. Steamer 'Water Witch' in Ossabaw Sound, Georgia, June 2-3, 1863," *The Georgia Historical Quarterly Vol. 3 No. 1* (March 1919), 12-13.

[62] Lamas, 37.

[63] Lamas, 36.

[64] Stoddard, 39.

[65] Lamas, 37-38

[66] Smith, 83, 125; Stoddard, 39.

[67] Rubin, 110.

[68] Lamas, 38.

[69] Rubin, 110; Lamas, 38; Kenneth W. Byrd, *Georgia Historical Markers-Coastal Counties* (Atlanta:
Cherokee Publishing Company, 1991), 21; Jim Miles, *Civil War Sites in Georgia* (Nashville: Rutledge Hill Press, 1996), 193.

[70] Miles, 193.

[71] *Insurance Maps of Thunderbolt, Georgia, 1888* (New York: Sanborn Map & Publishing Company, Ltd., 1888) (hereafter referred to as Sanborn Insurance Map, 1888), GHS.

[72] *Insurance Maps of Thunderbolt, Georgia, 1898* (New York: Sanborn Map & Publishing Company, Ltd., 1898) (hereafter referred to as Sanborn Insurance Map, 1898), GHS. See Chapter Seven for a thorough discussion of Thunderbolt's tourist sites.

[73] Sylvia Wood, "Interesting Firsts of Thunderbolt," *The Thunderbolt Vol. 1 No. 2* (4 March 1956), 8; Sylvia Wood, "Our Government," *The Thunder-*

bolt Vol. 1 No. 3 (16 March 1956), 1.

[74] Sylvia Wood, "Interesting Firsts of Thunderbolt," *The Thunderbolt Vol. 1 No. 2* (4 March 1956), 8.

[75] "Christianity in Thunderbolt," *The Thunderbolt Vol. 1 No. 5* (27 April 1956), 2; Whitson, 24; "Thunderbolt, Georgia Centennial 1856-1956," (2-5 March 1956, Official Program), 46; *Thunderbolt Vertical File*, GHS.

[76] Louise Ambos Wood and Elizabeth T. Holloway, "A Brief Resume of Christianity in Thunderbolt," 4. For more information on the history of the churches in Thunderbolt see Appendix A: Thunderbolt Area Churches.

[77] Kenneth W. Byrd, *Georgia Historical Markers: Coastal Counties* (Atlanta: Cherokee Publishing Company, 1991), 82; *Thunderbolt Vertical File*, GHS; Mary Beth D'Alonzo, *Streetcars of Chatham County* (Charleston: Arcadia Publishing, 1999), 43; Hazel Thomson, resident of Thunderbolt, interview by author, 20 March 2002, Thunderbolt, Georgia.

[78] "Thunderbolt, Georgia Centennial 1856-1956," 26; Byrd, 82; DeBolt, 93.

[79] Tabby was a common building material in coastal Georgia. It is a type of concrete made of crushed oyster shells.

[80] "Thunderbolt, Georgia Centennial 1856-1956," 26; Sanborn Insurance Map, 1898.

[81] "Thunderbolt, Georgia Centennial 1856-1956," 26.

[82] "Thunderbolt, Georgia Centennial 1856-1956," 26.

[83] Whitson, 24; *Thunderbolt Vertical File*, GHS; Stoddard, 36, 43.

[84] Stoddard, 36.

[85] Sanborn Insurance Map, 1898.

[86] Roger Williams," Savannah Yacht and Country Club's New Home Builds a Stronger Impetus to Local Sailing," *Savannah Morning News* (30 July 1950), 10; *"Savannah Yacht Club"* (1969), 4; W. G. Sutlive, "Savannah Yacht Club," *Outing, The Magazine of Amateur Sport and Pastime Vol. 23 No. 5* (February 1899), 458.

[87] DeBolt, 117; *Savannah Yacht Club* (Savannah: Braid & Hutton, 1905); Savannah Yacht Club (1969), 4; Gary L. Doster, *Southeast Georgia in Vintage Postcards* (Charleston: Arcadia Publishing, 1998), 122; *Thunderbolt Vertical File*, GHS; *Rules and Regulations of the Savannah Yacht Club 1886 (*George N. Nichols, Printer & Binder, 1886), 29; D'Alonzo, 39; W. G. Sutlive,, 458, 461; Sanborn Insurance Map, 1898; *Insurance Maps of Thunderbolt, Georgia, 1916* (New York: Sanborn Map & Publishing Company, Ltd., 1916) (hereafter referred to as Sanborn Insurance Map, 1916), GHS.

[88] Doster, 119; Georgia Historical Society Postcard Collection VM 1361 PC (hereafter referred to as VM 1361 PC), Box 8, GHS; W. G. Sutlive, 458, 461; Sanborn Insurance Maps, 1898, 1916.

[89] "Savannah Yacht Club," (1969), 4; Floyd, 1; "Thunderbolt Casino

Completely Destroyed by Devastating Blaze," Walter C. Hartridge Collection MS 1349 (hereafter referred to as MS 1349), Box 49, Folder 985, GHS; W. G. Sutlive, 459, 460.

[90] DeBolt, 117; "Map of Thunderbolt, 1976," (T. M. Reed, 1976); "Lilley Purchaser of Shrine Club," *Savannah Evening Press* (2 March 1944), MS 1349, Box 59, Folder 985, GHS; "Thunderbolt Casino Completely Destroyed by Devastating Blaze," MS 1349, Box 59, Folder 985, GHS.

[91] D'Alonzo, 7, 17; Henry Eason, *The Savannah Electric and Power Company 1866-1971* (Savannah: 1971), 11.

[92] Florence Olmstead, "Old City and Suburban Car Lines," *The Georgia Historical Quarterly Vol. 28 No. 3* (September 1944), 140.

[93] D'Alonzo, 27; "Queries and Answers," *The Georgia Historical Quarterly Vol. 1 No. 3*, 276; "A Map of 100 Square Miles Around Savannah," MS 1018, Vol. 2, Plate 36, GHS.

[94] Savannah Electric and Power Company Albums Collection VM 1381 (hereafter referred to as VM 1381), Album 4, GHS.

[95] Louise Johnson.

[96] D'Alonzo, 126; Louise Johnson.

[97] City and Suburban Railway Company Collection MS 147, Box 2, Folder 20, GHS; D'Alonzo, 10; *Thunderbolt Vertical File*, GHS.

[98] *Thunderbolt Vertical File*, GHS; "Work Starts on Casino Golf Course," MS 1349, Box 49, Folder 985, GHS; 1361 PC, Box 8, GHS; Doster, 121; VM 1381, Album 4, GHS.

[99] Eason, 32.

[100] "Likely Rebuild Casino," MS 1349, Box 49, Folder 985, GHS.

[101] *Thunderbolt Vertical File*, GHS; 1361 PC, Box 8, GHS; VM 1381, Album 4, GHS; "Thunderbolt Casino Completely Destroyed by Devastating Blaze," MS 1349, Box 49, Folder 985, GHS; Doster, 120.

[102] Georgia Historical Society Photograph Collection 1361 PH (hereafter referred to as 1361 PH), Folder 11, Item 3560, GHS; 1361 PC, Box 8, GHS; "Likely Rebuild Casino," MS 1349, Box 49, Folder 985, GHS; Sanborn Insurance Map, 1916.

[103] Eason, 32-33.

[104] "Likely Rebuild Casino," MS 1349, Box 49, Folder 985, GHS; D'Alonzo, 38; "Clubhouse at Recreation Center Burns," MS 1349, Box 49, Folder 985, GHS; "Thunderbolt Casino Completely Destroyed by Devastating Blaze," MS 1349, Box 49, Folder 985, GHS; "Work Starts on Casino Golf Course," MS 1349, Box 49, Folder 985, GHS.

[105] *Savannah Morning News* (3 November 1930), 10; "Thunderbolt Casino Completely Destroyed by Devastating Blaze," MS 1349, Box 49, Folder 985, GHS; "Likely Rebuild on Casino Golf Course," MS 1349, Box 49, Folder 985, GHS.

[106] "Bannon Lodge, Famous Eating Place, Reopens," *Savannah Morning News* (1 March 1948)MS 1349, Box 49, Folder 985, GHS; *Thunderbolt Vertical File*, GHS; "Bannon Home at Thunderbolt Sold," MS 1349, Box 49, Folder 985, GHS.

[107] Doster, 122; Cliff Sewell, "The Age of Pavilions," *Savannah Morning News Magazine* (4 October 1964), 6; Sanborn Insurance Maps, 1898, 1916.

[108] "Bannon Home at Thunderbolt Sold," MS 1349, Box 49, Folder 985, GHS; "Bannon Lodge Coming Down," *Savannah Evening Press* (4 March 1939), MS 1349, Box 59, Folder 985, GHS; "James E. Bannon Dies in Savannah," *Savannah Morning News* (20 December 1941), MS 1349, Folder 1418, GHS; "Bannon Lodge, Famous Eating Place, Reopens," MS 1349, Folder 1418, GHS.

[109] "Bannon Lodge Coming Down," *Savannah Evening Press* (4 March 1939), MS 1349, Box 59, Folder 985, GHS; "James E. Bannon Dies in Savannah," *Savannah Morning News* (20 December 1941), MS 1349, Folder 1418, GHS.

[110] "Bannon Home at Thunderbolt Sold," MS 1349, Box 49, Folder 985, GHS; "Bannon Residence Will Become Home for Elderly People," *Savannah Morning News* (11 January 1949).

[111] "Bannon Home at Thunderbolt Sold," MS 1349, Box 49, Folder 985, GHS; "Bannon Residence Will Become Home for Elderly People," *Savannah Morning News* (11 January 1949); *Insurance Maps of Thunderbolt, Georgia, 1950* (New York: Sanborn Map & Publishing Company, Ltd., 1950) (hereafter referred to as Sanborn Insurance Map, 1950), GHS.

[112] Whitson, 24; D'Alonzo, 41; *Michael J. Doyle*, GBS Notebooks, GHS; B. A. Gilreath, "History of Thunderbolt," (Private collection of Hazel Thomson, Thunderbolt, Georgia), 2; Sanborn Insurance Map, 1898.

[113] D'Alonzo, 41; Whitson, 24; "The Chatham Hunt Club, Horse Show and Race Meet, 1909," Program (Savannah: M.S. & D.A. Byck Company, Printers, 1909); Gilreath, 2; Joe Wilharm, resident of Thunderbolt, interview by author, 23 March 2002, Thunderbolt, Georgia; Stoddard, 43.

[114] Alice Johnson, resident of Thunderbolt, phone interview by author, February 2002, Thunderbolt, Georgia; Joan Cesaroni-Counsil, native of Thunderbolt, interview by author, 20 February 2002, Savannah, Georgia; Gilreath, 2.

[115] Frank T. Wheeler, *The Savannah Races* (Dover: Arcadia Publishing, 1998), 9.

[116] Wheeler, *The Savannah Races*, 10; DeBolt, 120.

[117] Wheeler, *The Savannah Races*, 24, 33.

[118] Wheeler, *The Savannah Races*, 27, 31, 32, 35; DeBolt, 120.

[119] Wheeler, *The Savannah Races*, 35; Wilharm interview.

[120] Wheeler, *The Savannah Races*, 38.

[121] Wheeler, *The Savannah Races*, 43, 45, 50.

[122] Wheeler, *The Savannah Races*, 58.

[123] Whitson, 44.

[124] "The Five Elected Mayors of Thunderbolt," *The Thunderbolt Vol. 1 No. 2* (4 March 1956), 5; Sylvia Wood, "Our Government," *The Thunderbolt Vol. 1 No. 3* (16 March 1956), 1; Sylvia Wood, "The Naming of Thunderbolt," *The Thunderbolt Vol. 1 No. 1* (19 February 1956), 3; "Thunderbolt, Georgia Centennial 1856-1956," 34; John Sutlive, "The Casino, Thunderbolt, Georgia, 1975," (TMs, photocopy), *Thunderbolt Clipping File*, Bull Street Library, 1.

[125] *The Thunderbolt Vol. 1 No. 2* (4 March 1956), 3; Whitson, 44.

[126] "Thunderbolt's Town Hall is Finished," *Savannah Morning News* (2 June 1914); *The Thunderbolt Museum Society Newsletter Vol. 1 Issue 1* (Spring 2001), 1; *Thunderbolt Vertical File*, GHS.

[127] "Thunderbolt's Town Hall is Finished," *Savannah Morning News* (2 June 1914); VM 1361 PH, Box 17, Folder 11, Item 3559, GHS.

[128] Whitson, 44.

[129] Whitson, 44; *Savannah Newspaper Digest 1936-1937* (11 August 1936), GHS; "Bonds Win Easily in Thunderbolt," MS 1349, GHS.

[130] *The Thunderbolt Museum Society Newsletter Vol. 1 Issue 1* (Spring 2001), 1; Loring Horne, native of Thunderbolt, interview by author, 23 March 2002, Wilmington Island, Georgia; George Oliver Mulligan, Jr., resident of Thunderbolt, interview by author, 23 March 2002, Wilmington Island, Georgia.

[131] "Asa Candler, Jr., Buys Casino Site," MS 1349, Box 49, Folder 985, GHS; *Savannah Morning News* (25 May 1939), 16; *Savannah Morning News* (17 June 1939), 12.

[132] "Asa Candler, Jr., Buys Casino Site," MS 1349, Box 49, Folder 985, GHS; Savannah Morning News (3 November 1939), 18; "Gala Day Celebration, Yacht Basin at Thunderbolt, November 2, 1939," (Program), *Thunderbolt Vertical File*, GHS, 5; "Map of Thunderbolt, 1976," (T. M. Reed, 1976); "Yacht Basin as a Navy Shelter," *Savannah Morning News*, MS 1349, Box 49, Folder 985, GHS.

[133] "Contract Let for Yacht Basin Here," MS 1349, Box 49, Folder 985, GHS; "Yacht Basin as a Navy Shelter," *Savannah Morning News*, MS 1349, Box 49, Folder 985, GHS.

[134] *Savannah Morning News* (4 November 1941), 16; "Thunderbolt Yacht Basin Dissolved," *Savannah Evening Press* (15 October 1942); "Yacht Basin as a Navy Shelter," *Savannah Morning News*, MS 1349, Box 49, Folder 985, GHS; *Savannah Morning News* (22 July 1944), MS 1349, Box 49, Folder 985, GHS.

[135] Stoddard, 50; "Thunderbolt, Georgia Centennial 1856-1956," 31; *Sa-*

vannah Newspaper Digest 1950 (1 May 1950), GHS; John Sutlive, 2.

[136] Joan Cesaroni-Counsil interview.

[137] Stoddard, 36, 38, 48; Sanborn Insurance Map, 1916.

[138] Sanborn Insurance Map, 1916.

[139] Grover Ables, "Trawlers at Thunderbolt Refurbished for Big Day," *Savannah Morning News* (3 April 1949); "Industrial Savannah: No. 39 The Fishing Industry," *Savannah Morning News* (20 April 1925), 7.

[140] "Savannah-Leading Distribution Point for the Sea Food Trade in the Southeast," *The Fish and Oyster Reporter* (May 1926), 6; *Fish and Shellfish Vertical File*, GHS; "Industrial Savannah: No. 39 The Fishing Industry," 7.

[141] "Gala Day Celebration, Yacht Basin at Thunderbolt, 1939," 5; "Savannah-Leading Distribution Point for the Sea Food Trade in the Southeast," 6.

[142] "Thunderbolt, Georgia Centennial 1856-1956," 18; Wylly Folk St. John, "Old World Ceremony Echoed at Thunderbolt in Blessing of the Shrimp Fleet," *Atlanta Journal and Constitution Magazine* (19 July 1951), 6.

[143] Loring Horne interview; Gilbert Maggioni, Interview by Remer Young Lane (n.d.), Remer Young Lane Collection MS 2129 (hereafter called MS 2129), Box 1, GHS; "Georgia's Seafood Industries Are Picturesque and Profitable," *Georgia Progress Vol. 4 No. 9* (March 1948), 2; Frank T. Wheeler, "Working the Catch: Coastal Georgia's Seafood Industry and Its Biracial Labor Force," *The Georgia Historical Quarterly Vol. 81 No. 2* (1997), 491; Sanborn Insurance Map, 1950.

[144] "Georgia's Seafood Industries Are Picturesque and Profitable," 3.

[145] "Georgia's Seafood Industries Are Picturesque and Profitable," 1, 2; Loring Horne interview.

[146] "Georgia's Seafood Industries Are Picturesque and Profitable," 2; "Industrial Savannah: No. 39 The Fishing Industry," 7.

[147] Loring Horne interview; "Georgia's Seafood Industries Are Picturesque and Profitable," 4; *Thunderbolt Clipping File*, Bull Street Library.

[148] "Georgia's Seafood Industries Are Picturesque and Profitable," 2; Joan Cesaroni-Counsil interview.

[149] Al Lanier, "Thunderbolt Fleet Heads South to Cash in on Shrimp Bonanza," *Savannah Morning News* (13 February 1950), 14.

[150] St. John, 6.

[151] St. John, 6.

[152] *Joseph Cannarella*, GBS Notebooks, GHS; A. C. Mathews, Jr., "Columns to Monuments," *Savannah Morning News* (November), 12, 13, *Thunderbolt Vertical File*, GHS; Louis C. Mathews, Interview by Remer Young Lane (December 1976), MS 2129, Box 1, GHS.

[153] Mathews, 12, 13, *Thunderbolt Vertical File*, GHS; Louis C. Mathews, Interview by Remer Young Lane (December 1976), MS 2129, Box 1, GHS.

[154] Ables.

[155] Mathews, 12, 13; *Thunderbolt Vertical File*, GHS.

[156] Gilbert Maggioni, Interview by Remer Young Lane (n.d.), MS 2129, Box 1, GHS; Wheeler, "Working the Catch," 486; "Maggioni, Company Observe Eightieth Year of Operation," *Savannah Morning News* (15 January 1950); "Georgia's Industries Are Picturesque and Profitable," 1.

[157] "Georgia's Industries Are Picturesque and Profitable," 1; Wheeler, "Working the Catch," 487, 493; "Maggioni, Company Observe Eightieth Year of Operation,"; Gilbert Maggioni, Interview by Remer Young Lane (n.d.), MS 2129, Box 1, GHS.

[158] Wheeler, "Working the Catch," 487; Gilbert Maggioni, Interview by Remer Young Lane (n.d.), MS 2129, Box 1, GHS; "Maggioni, Company Observe Eightieth Year of Operation"; "Georgia's Industries Are Picturesque and Profitable," 1; Joan Cesaroni-Counsil interview.

[159] Wheeler, "Working the Catch," 487; "Maggioni, Company Observe Eightieth Year of Operation"; Joan Cesaroni-Counsil interview.

[160] Cordray-Foltz Photograph Collection VM 1360 PH (hereafter referred to as VM 1360 PH), Box 17, Folder 3, GHS; Mathews, 13; *Thunderbolt Vertical File*, GHS; Gilbert Maggioni, Interview by Remer Young Lane (n.d.), MS 2129, Box 1, GHS; D'Alonzo, 42; WPA, 262.

[161] WPA, 262; Joan Cesaroni-Counsil; Wheeler, "Working the Catch," 487, 492, 494.

[162] Wheeler, "Working the Catch," 490.

[163] *Thunderbolt Vertical File*, GHS; "Ambos is Honored as Dean of Fishermen," *Savannah Evening Press* (7 April 1949), *Thunderbolt Vertical File*, GHS; Joan Cesaroni-Counsil interview; Loring Horne interview; Stoddard, 48.

[164] *Thunderbolt Vertical File*, GHS; "Ambos is Honored as Dean of Fishermen."

[165] "Thunderbolt," *Savannah News Press* (8 August 1993); Joan Cesaroni-Counsil interview; "Trade Winds Company Adds Second Shrimp Packing Plant," *Savannah Morning News* (11 September 1950), 16.

[166] "Trade Winds Company Adds Second Shrimp Packing Plant," 16.

[167] William Mullis later sold his interest in the business to Henry Ambos and opened Neptunalia packing plant on Victory Drive, marketing his line under the brand name Gold King. He later expanded into the retail business with the Neptunalia Restaurant (Gilreath, 2).

[168] "Trade Winds Company Adds Second Shrimp Packing Plant," 16; Ables.

[169] "Trade Winds Company Adds Second Shrimp Packing Plant," 16.

[170] "Trade Winds Company Adds Second Shrimp Packing Plant," 16.

[171] "Trade Winds Company Adds Second Shrimp Packing Plant," 16;

Thunderbolt Vertical File, GHS.

[172] Joan Cesaroni-Counsil interview.

[173] Joan Cesaroni-Counsil interview; Sanborn Insurance Maps, 1916, 1950.

[174] Joan Cesaroni-Counsil interview.

[175] Joe Ledlie, "Damages in Blaze: $30,000," *Savannah Evening Press* (22 June 1966).

[176] Mathews, 13.

[177] Joan Cesaroni-Counsil interview; Mathews, 13; *Thunderbolt Vertical File*, GHS.

[178] Mathews, 13; "Park Dedication Readied," *Savannah Morning News* (17 October 1971).

[179] "Park Dedication Readied."

[180] Raffaele Manzi, *The Italian-American Experience* (New Jersey: Means, Inc., 1994), 43.

[181] St. John, 6; Father Robert J. Teoli, "An Explanation of the Blessing," *Thunderbolt Vertical File*, GHS; "Thunderbolt, Georgia Centennial 1856-1956," 42.

[182] Teoli, "An Explanation of the Blessing."

[183] "Thunderbolt to Plan Blessing of Fleet at Meeting Tonight," *Savannah Morning News* (11 March 1949); "Blessing of Fleet Ceremony Observed in Thunderbolt," *Savannah Evening Press* (9 June 1969), 12.

[184] Teoli, "An Explanation of the Blessing."

[185] "Rulers of the Fleet will be Selected," *Savannah Evening Press* (15 March 1949); "Blessing of the Fleet is Scheduled Today; King, Queen Crowned," *Savannah Morning News* (10 April 1949); "Blessing of Fleet Colorful Rite," *Savannah Evening Press* (11 April 1949), 8; Millard Shepherd, "Thunderbolt Fleet Blessed with Impressive Ceremonies," *Savannah Morning News* (11 June 1951); "Blessing of Fleet Ceremony Observed in Thunderbolt," 12.

[186] "Fleet will get Blessing June 14," *Savannah Evening Press* (6 June 1970); "Blessing of Fleet Colorful Rite," 8; "Map of Thunderbolt, Georgia," (T. M. Reed, 1976); Ables.

[187] *Savannah Evening Press* (7 June 1969), *Thunderbolt Clipping File*, Bull Street Library; Joan Cesaroni-Counsil interview; "Blessing of the Fleet is Scheduled Today; King, Queen Crowned."

[188] Joan Cesaroni-Counsil interview; "Map of Thunderbolt, Georgia," (T. M. Reed, 1976); Reuben Ware, "Thunderbolt," music and lyrics (1976).

[189] Whitson, 38; "Thunderbolt Plans Centennial," *The Thunderbolt Vol. 1 No. 1* (19 February 1956), 1, 3.

[190] "Thunderbolt Plans Centennial," 1, 3.

[191] "Prince Preston to Speak Saturday," *The Thunderbolt Vol. 1 No. 2* (4 March 1956), 1; "The Church Marches On," *The Thunderbolt Vol. 1 No. 2* (4

March 1956), 1.

[192] Myrtle Baulkmon, resident of Thunderbolt, Phone interview by author (April 2002), Thunderbolt, Georgia.

[193] Myrtle Baulkmon.

[194] Myrtle Baulkmon.

[195] Elizabeth Ward, native of Thunderbolt, Phone interview by author (April 2002), Thunderbolt, Georgia.

[196] Elizabeth Ward.

[197] Louise Johnson, resident of Thunderbolt, Phone interview by author (April 2002), Thunderbolt, Georgia; Myrtle Baulkmon.

[198] Louise Johnson.

[199] Lola Dixon, resident of Thunderbolt, Interview by author (April 2002), Thunderbolt, Georgia; Mrs. Myrtice Lewis, native of Thunderbolt, Phone Interview by author (April 2002), Thunderbolt, Georgia; Myrtle Baulkmon.

[200] Mrs. Myrtice Lewis; Lola Dixon.

[201] Mrs. Myrtice Lewis; Lola Dixon; Myrtle Baulkmon.

[202] Lola Dixon; Mrs. Myrtice Lewis; Myrtle Baulkmon.

[203] Mrs. Myrtice Lewis; *Thunderbolt Vertical File,* GHS; Hall, 189; Lola Dixon.

[204] Louise Johnson.

[205] Lola Dixon.

[206] Louise Johnson.

[207] Myrtle Baulkmon.

[208] Myrtle Baulkmon; Louise Johnson; Unknown Thunderbolt Resident, "Thunderbolt Old Timers Reunion" (23 March 2002), Wilmington Island, Georgia.

[209] Mrs. Myrtice Lewis.

[210] Mrs. Myrtice Lewis.

[211] "Suburban News," *The Savannah Tribune* (regular column throughout the 1940s and 1950s); Rev. Leonard Smalls, minister of Litway Baptist Church, Phone interview by author (April 2002), Thunderbolt, Georgia.

[212] Rev. Leonard Smalls.

[213] Rev. Leonard Smalls.

[214] Rev. Leonard Smalls.

[215] Lindsey Logan, "Thunderbolt Tradition Ends, Ambos Brothers Selling Property," (courtesy of Joan Cesaroni-Counsil); Brian R. Bishop, "Thunderbolt Monument Honors Town's Fishing Legacy," *Savannah Morning News* (3 June 1996), 1A.

[216] Joan Cesaroni-Counsil interview.

[217] "Thunderbolt," *Savannah Evening Press* (8 August 1993).

[218] "Thunderbolt"; Logan.

[219] "The Fishermen's Memorial," (Savannah: A. M. Edwards & Son Print-

ing Company, 1996).

[220] "The Fishermen's Memorial"; Bishop, 1A.

[221] *Savannah Morning News* (12 March 1998), *Thunderbolt Vertical File*, GHS.

[222] *The Thunderbolt Museum Society Newsletter Vol. 1 Issue 1* (Spring 2001), 1; Ann Marshall, "Thunderbolt Plans Municipal Building," *Savannah Evening Press* (9 January 1969); "Thunderbolt Hall Opens," *Savannah Morning News* (10 May 1973), 8D.

[223] *Savannah Morning News* (11 September 2001), 13A; Tasha Gatlin, "What is that Construction Project?" *Savannah Morning News* (4 February 2000), 2; "Old Thunderbolt Town Hall on the Move," *Savannah Evening Press* (24 June 1988).

[224] *The Thunderbolt Vol. 1 No. 1* (19 February 1956), 2; Louis Ambos Wood & Elizabeth T. Holloway, "A Brief Resume of Christianity in Thunderbolt," 4.

[225] *The Thunderbolt Vol. 1 No. 1* (19 February 1956), 3; Wood & Holloway, 10.

[226] *The Thunderbolt Vol. 1 No. 1* (19 February 1956), 3; *The Thunderbolt Museum Society Newsletter Vol. 1 Issue 1* (Spring 2001); Whitson, 24; Wood & Holloway, 8; Louise Ambos Wood, "A Brief History of Saint Luke's Lutheran Church, 1930-1965."

[227] "Sunset Baptist Church Formed," *The Thunderbolt Vol. 1 No. 1* (19 February 1956), 1; "Sunset Church in New Building," *The Thunderbolt Vol. 1 No. 6* (8 June 1956), 3.

[228] *The Thunderbolt Vol. 1 No. 1* (19 February 1956), 3, 7; Wood & Holloway, 11.

[229] *The Thunderbolt Vol. 1 No. 1* (19 February 1956), 3; *Savannah Morning News* (2 February 1963), *Thunderbolt Clipping File*, Bull Street Library; Wood & Holloway, 6, 7.

[230] "Christianity in Thunderbolt," *The Thunderbolt Vol. 1 No. 5*, 2; Whitson, 24, 44; Wood & Holloway, 3.

[231] *The Thunderbolt Vol. 1 No. 1* (19 February 1956), 3; Whitson, 24; Wood & Holloway, 5.

[232] "Thunderbolt," *Savannah Morning News Magazine* (July 1973), 4, *Thunderbolt Clipping File*, Bull Street Library.

Bibliography

Primary Sources

Baulkmon, Myrtle, resident of Thunderbolt. Phone interview by author, April 2002, Thunderbolt, Georgia.

"The Chatham Hunt Club, Horse Show and Race Meet, 1909." Savannah: M.S. & D.A. Byck Company, Printers, 1909.

City and Suburban Railway Company Collection MS 147, Box 2, Folder 20, Items 901-902. Georgia Historical Society, Savannah, Georgia.

Cordray-Foltz Photograph Collection VM 1360 PH, Box 3, Folders 23-29; Box 16, Folders 10-25; Box 17, Folders 1-4; Box 22, Folders 3-4, 6-15, 22-26; Box 26, Folders 21-23; Box 27. Georgia Historical Society, Savannah, Georgia.

Counsil, Joan Cesaroni, native of Thunderbolt. Interview by author, February 2002, Savannah, Georgia.

Dixon, Lola, resident of Thunderbolt. Interview by author, April 2002, Thunderbolt, Georgia.

"Gala Day Celebration: Yacht Basin at Thunderbolt, 1939." (Program). Georgia Historical Society, Savannah, Georgia.

Georgia Historical Society Photograph Collection VM 1361PH, Box 17, Folder 11; Box 20, Folder 5; Box 22; Box 27, Folder 8; Box 28; Box 29, Folder 11. Georgia Historical Society, Savannah, Georgia.

Georgia Historical Society Postcard Collection VM 1361PC, Boxes 6 and 8. Georgia Historical Society, Savannah, Georgia.

Georgia Historical Society Print Collection VM 1361PR, Boxes 2, 3, and 4. Georgia Historical Society, Savannah, Georgia.

"Georgia's Seafood Industries are Picturesque and Profitable." *Georgia Progress Vol. IV, No. 9* (March 1948).

Horne, Loring, native of Thunderbolt. Interview by author, March 2002, Wilmington Island, Georgia.

Insurance Maps of Thunderbolt, Georgia, 1888, 1898, 1916, 1950. New York: Sanborn Map & Publishing Company, Ltd., 1888, 1898, 1916, 1950. Georgia Historical Society, Savannah, Georgia.

Johnson, Alice, resident of Thunderbolt. Phone interview by author, February 2002, Thunderbolt, Georgia.

Johnson, Louise, resident of Thunderbolt. Phone interview by author, April 2002, Thunderbolt, Georgia.

Julien K. Quattlebaum Collection MS 2168. Georgia Historical Society, Savannah, Georgia.

Lewis, Mrs. Myrtice, native of Thunderbolt. Phone interview by author, April 2002, Thunderbolt, Georgia.

"Map of Thunderbolt, Georgia, 1976." T. M. Reed, 1976.

Mulligan, George Oliver, Jr., resident of Thunderbolt. Interview by author, March 2002, Wilmington Island, Georgia.

Remer Young Lane Collection MS 2129, Box 1, Folders 2-4. Georgia Historical Society, Savannah, Georgia.

Rules and Regulations of the Savannah Yacht Club, 1886. Savannah: George N. Nichols, Printer and Binder, 1886.

"Savannah and Its Environs 1733-1903 Vol. I-III." Waring Map Collection, MS 1018. Georgia Historical Society, Savannah, Georgia.

Savannah Electric and Power Albums Collection VM 1381, Album 4. Georgia Historical Society, Savannah, Georgia.

"Savannah-Leading Distribution Point for the Sea Food Trade in the Southeast." *The Fish and Oyster Reporter* (May 1926): 6.

Savannah Yacht Club. Savannah: Braid and Hutton, 1905.

"Savannah Yacht Club." Savannah: Savannah Yacht Club, 1969. *Yacht Club Vertical File.* Georgia Historical Society, Savannah, Georgia.

Smalls, Reverend Leonard, minister of Litway Baptist Church. Phone interview by author, April 2002, Thunderbolt, Georgia.

Sutlive, W. G. "Savannah Yacht Club." *Outing, the Magazine of Amateur Sport and Pastime Vol. XXXIII No. 5* (February 1899).

Thomson, Hazel, resident of Thunderbolt. Interview by author, March 2002, Thunderbolt, Georgia.

Walter C. Hartridge Collection MS 1349, Box 59, Folders 985 and 1418; Box 74, Folder 1418. Georgia Historical Society, Savannah, Georgia.

Ward, Elizabeth, native of Thunderbolt. Phone interview by author, April 2002, Thunderbolt, Georgia.

Ware, Reuben. "Thunderbolt: A Song about the Activities of the Blessing of the Fleet." Words and Music. 1976.

Wilharm, Joe, native of Thunderbolt. Interview by author, March 2002, Wilmington Island, Georgia.

Secondary Sources

Ables, Grover. "Trawlers at Thunderbolt Refurbished for Big Day." *Savannah Morning News* (3 April 1949).

Bell, Laura Palmer. "A New Theory on the Plan of Savannah." *The Georgia Historical Quarterly Vol. XLVIII No. 2* (June 1964): 147-165.

Bishop, Brian R. "Honoring Aunt Nellie." *Savannah Morning News* (16 June 1996).

———— "Thunderbolt Monument Honors Town's Fishing Legacy." *Savannah Morning News* (3 June 1996): 1A.

Boats and Racing Vertical File. Georgia Historical Society, Savannah, Georgia.

Bonaventure Historical Society. *Bonaventure Cemetery, Savannah, Georgia, Index Section A-H*. Savannah: Bonaventure Historical Society, Inc., 2000.

Bragg, Lillian Chaplin. "Cricket Farm at Thunderbolt, n.d." TMs (photocopy). Lillian Chaplin Bragg Papers Collection MS 83, Folder 94, Item 831. Georgia Historical Society, Savannah, Georgia.

Byrd, Kenneth W. *Georgia Historical Markers: Coastal Counties*. Atlanta: Cherokee Publishing Company, 1991.

Callaway, James Etheridge. *The Early Settlement of Georgia*. Athens: The University of Georgia Press, 1948.

"Cannarella, Joseph." GBS Notebooks. Georgia Historical Society, Savannah, Georgia.

"The Capture of the U.S. Steamer 'Water Witch' in Ossabaw Sound, Georgia, June 2-3, 1864." *The Georgia Historical Quarterly Vol. 3 No. 1* (March 1919): 11.

Coulter, E. Merton and Albert B. Saye, eds. *A List of the Early Settlers of Georgia*. Athens: The University of Georgia Press, 1949.

Coulter, E. Merton, ed. *The Journal of William Stephens, 1743-1745, Vol. I*. Athens: The University of Georgia Press, 1958.

——— *The Journal of William Stephens, 1743-1745, Vol. II*. Athens: The University of Georgia Press, 1959.

D'Alonzo, Mary Beth. *Streetcars of Chatham County*. Charleston: Arcadia Publishing, 1999.

Daniels, Ann Marshall. "Construction Crew Uncovers Old Skeletons in Thunderbolt." *Savannah Evening Press* (5 May 1977).

Darby, Betty. "Thunderbolt New Bridge, Library On Way." *Savannah News Press* (8 February 1987).

Davis, Curtis Carroll. "Dr. Caruthers Confronts the Bureaucrats." *The Geor-*

gia Historical Quarterly Vol. LVI No. 1 (Spring 1972): 101-111.

Davis, Harold E. *The Fledgling Province: Social and Cultural Life in Colonial Georgia, 1733-1776.* Chapel Hill: The University of North Carolina Press, 1976.

DeBolt, Margaret Wayt. *Savannah: A Historical Portrait.* Virginia Beach: The Donning Company, Publishers, Inc., 1976.

DeBrahm, John Gerar William. *History of the Province of Georgia with Maps of Original Surveys.* Wormsloe: 1899.

Doster, Gary L. *Southeast Georgia in Vintage Postcards.* Charleston: Arcadia Publishing, 1998.

"Doyle, Michael J." GBS Notebooks. Georgia Historical Society, Savannah, Georgia.

Eason, Henry. *The Savannah Electric and Power Company 1866-1971.* Savannah: 1971.

Fish and Shellfish Vertical File. Georgia Historical Society, Savannah, Georgia.

The Fishermen's Memorial. Savannah: A. M. Edwards & Son Printing Company, 1996.

Floyd, M. H. and D. B. "Thunderbolt, n.d." TMs (photocopy). M. H. and D. B. Floyd Papers, MS #1308, Box 41, Item #529. Georgia Historical Society, Savannah, Georgia.

Freeman, Ron. *Savannah People, Places and Events.* Savannah: H. Ronald Freeman, 1997.

Gatlin, Tasha. "What is That Construction Project." *Savannah Morning News* (4 February 2000): 2.

Gilreath, B. A. "History of Thunderbolt." TMs (photocopy). Private Collection of Hazel Thomson. Thunderbolt, Georgia.

Granger, Mary, ed. *Savannah River Plantations.* Savannah Writers' Project. Savannah: Georgia Historical Society, 1947.

Hall, Clyde W. One Hundred Years of Educating at Savannah State College 1890-1990. East Peoria: Versa Press, Inc., 1991.

Harden, William. *A History of Savannah and South Georgia, Vol. I.* Atlanta: Cherokee Publishing Company, 1969.

———— *Recollections of a Long and Satisfactory Life.* Savannah: Review Printing Company, Inc., 1934.

Hodlee, Thomas W. and Howard A. Schretter. The Atlas of Georgia. Athens: The University of Georgia Press, 1986.

Horses Vertical File. Georgia Historical Society, Savannah, Georgia.

Kelly, Patrick. "Thunderbolt Holds Charm, Quaintness." *Savannah Morning News* (31 March 1962).

Kilbourne, Elizabeth Evans. *Savannah, Georgia, Newspaper Clippings (Georgia Gazette) Vol. I, 1763-1770.* Savannah: Elizabeth Evans Kilbourne, 1998.

———— *Savannah, Georgia, Newspaper Clippings (Georgia Gazette) Vol. II, 1774-1785.* Savannah: Elizabeth Evans Kilbourne, 1999.

———— *Savannah, Georgia, Newspaper Clippings (Georgia Gazette) Vol. III, 1786-1792.* Savannah: Elizabeth Evans Kilbourne, 2000.

Lacey Biography File. Georgia Historical Society, Savannah, Georgia.

Lamas, Claudia B. "Fortification Survey of Savannah River and Area Waterways, Savannah, Georgia 1861-1865." TMs (photocopy). Minis Room, Lane Library, Armstrong Atlantic State University, Savannah, Georgia.

Lane, Mills. *Savannah Revisited: History and Architecture.* Savannah: The Beehive Press, 1994.

Lanier, Al. "Thunderbolt Fleet Heads South to Cash In On Shrimp Bonanza." *Savannah Morning News* (13 February 1950): 14.

Ledlie, Joe. "Damages in Blaze: $30,000." *Savannah Evening Press* (22 June 1966).

Manzi, Raffaele. *The Italian-American Experience in Georgia.* New Jersey: Means, Inc., 1994.

Marshall, Ann. "Thunderbolt Plans Municipal Building." *Savannah Evening Press* (9 January 1969).

Mathews, A. C., Jr. "Columns to Monuments." *Savannah Morning News* (November): 12.

McPherson, Robert G., ed. *The Journal of the Earl of Egmont: Abstracts of the Trustees Proceedings for the Establishment of the Colony of Georgia, 1732-1733*. Athens: The University of Georgia Press, 1962.

Miles, Jim. *Civil War Sites in Georgia*. Nashville: Rutledge Hill Press, 1996.

Olmstead, Florence. "Old City and Suburban Car Lines." *The Georgia Historical Quarterly Vol. 28 No. 3* (September 1944): 138-140.

"Queries and Answers." *The Georgia Historical Quarterly Vol. I No. 3:* 275-76.

Rubin, Rabbi Saul Jacob. *Third to None, the Saga of Savannah Jewry, 1733-1983*. Savannah: The Congregation Mickve Israel, 1983.

Russell, Preston and Barbara Hines. *Savannah: A History of Her People Since 1733*. Savannah: Frederic C. Beil, Publishers, Inc., 1992.

Savannah Evening Press (Savannah, Georgia).

Savannah Morning News (Savannah, Georgia).

Savannah Newspaper Digests, 1929-1950. Georgia Historical Society, Savannah, Georgia.

Savannah Tribune (Savannah).

Savannah Unit, Federal Writers' Project, Works Progress Administration of Georgia. "Causton's Bluff, Deptford, Brewton Hill, Three Allied Plantations." *The Georgia Historical Quarterly Vol. 23 No. 1* (March 1939): 28-54.

Savannah Yacht Club Vertical File. Georgia Historical Society, Savannah, Georgia.

Sewell, Cliff. "The Age of Pavilions." *Savannah Morning News Magazine* (4 October 1964): 6-7.

Shearouse, E. L. "Southern History." *The Thunderbolt Vol. 1 No. 3* (16 March 1956): 2.

Shepherd, Millard. "Thunderbolt Fleet Blessed with Impressive Ceremonies." *Savannah Morning News* (11 June 1951).

Skutch, Jan. "First Cases Heard in New Facilities." *Savannah Evening* Press (6 June 1973).

Smith, Derek. *Civil War Savannah*. Savannah: Frederic C. Beil, Publishers, Inc., 1997.

"SSU History: A Brief History," http://www.savstate.edu/welcome/history.html, last updated November 1998, accessed 10 April 2002.

St. John, Wylly Folk. "Old World Ceremony Echoed at Thunderbolt in Blessing of the Shrimp Fleet." *Atlanta Journal and Constitution Magazine* (19 July 1951): 6.

Stoddard, Ann. "Thunderbolt, 1973." TMs (photocopy). Georgia Room, Bull Street Branch, Chatham-Effingham-Liberty Counties Library, Savannah, Georgia.

Sutlive, John. "The Casino, Thunderbolt, Georgia, 1975." TMs (photocopy). Thunderbolt Clipping File, Georgia Room, Bull Street Branch, Chatham-Effingham-Liberty Counties Library, Savannah, Georgia.

"Roger Hugh Lacey, the First Grand Master of Masons in Georgia." *Alee Temple Fez* (August 1961): 4.

The Thunderbolt (Thunderbolt, Georgia). 1956.

Thunderbolt Clipping File. Georgia Room, Bull Street Branch, Chatham-Effingham-Liberty County Libraries, Savannah, Georgia.

"Thunderbolt, Georgia Centennial 1856-1956." Official Program, 2-4 March 1956.

Thunderbolt Museum Society Scrapbook. Thunderbolt Museum Society, Thunderbolt, Georgia.

Thunderbolt Vertical File. Georgia Historical Society, Savannah, Georgia.

Toledano, Roulhac. *The National Trust Guide to Savannah*. New York: John Wiley and Sons, Inc., 1997.

Walck, Pamela E. "Thunderbolt Residents Rally Behind Their Library." *Savannah Morning News* (19 July 2001): C1.

Warren, Mary Bondurant and Jack Moreland Jones, eds. *Georgia Governor and Council Journals 1753-1760*. Danielsville: Hermitage Press, 1991.

———— *Georgia Governor and Council Journals 1761-1767*. Athens: Heritage Press, 1992.

Weeks, Carl Solana. *The Road to Revolution in Colonial Georgia: Savannah in the Time of Peter Tondee*. Columbia: Summerhouse Press, 1997.

Wheeler, Frank T. "Georgia History in Pictures: Working the Catch: Coastal Georgia's Seafood Industry and Its Biracial Labor Force." *The Georgia Historical Quarterly Vol. LXXXI No. 2* (Summer 1997): 485-497.

———— *The Savannah Races*. Dover: Arcadia Publishing, 1998.

Whitson, Vin. "History of Thunderbolt." *Thunderbolt, Georgia Centennial 1856-1956* (2-5 March 1956), Official Program.

Wilson, Adelaide. *Historic and Picturesque Savannah*. Boston: Boston Photogravure Company, 1889.

Wood, Louise Ambos and Elizabeth T. Holloway. "A Brief Resume of Christianity in Thunderbolt." Thunderbolt Museum Society Scrapbook.

Wood, Louise Ambos. "A Brief History of Saint Luke's Lutheran Church: November 9, 1930-November 7, 1965, 35th Anniversary." Thunderbolt Museum Society Scrapbook.

Wood, Sylvia. "Interesting Firsts of Thunderbolt." *The Thunderbolt Vol. 1 No. 2* (4 March 1956): 8.

———— "The Naming of Thunderbolt." *The Thunderbolt Vol. 1 No. 1* (19 February 1956): 3.

———— "Our Government." *The Thunderbolt Vol. 1 No. 3* (16 March 1956): 1.

Workers of the Writers' Program of the Works Progress Administration of the State of Georgia. *Georgia: The WPA Guide to its Towns and Countryside.* The University of South Carolina Press. Thunderbolt Museum Society Scrapbook.

Young, Roger W. "Two Years at Fort Barstow, 1862-1864." *The Georgia Historical Quarterly Vol. XXIII No. 3* (September 1939): 253-264.

Index

About the Author

Luciana Spracher works as a freelance researcher under the name Bricks and Bones Historical Research in Savannah, Georgia. Collaborating with a variety of public and private clients, she has worked to preserve the built environment through historical documentation. Her unique approach to Savannah's history combines architectural history, property research, and genealogy for a greater understanding of the relationship between people and the built environment. After receiving a bachelor's degree in historic preservation from Savannah College of Art and Design, she earned a master's degree in history from Armstrong Atlantic State University. Her published works include *Lost Savannah* (Arcadia, 2003).